THE CHILDREN'S HOUR:

Radio Programs for Children, 1929-1956

by

Marilyn Lawrence Boemer

The Scarecrow Press, Inc.
Metuchen, N.J., & London
1989

Library of Congress Cataloging-in-Publication Data

Boemer, Marilyn Lawrence
    The children's hour : radio programs for children, 1929-
1956 / by Marilyn Lawrence Boemer.
        p.   cm.
    Includes bibliographical references.
    ISBN 0-8108-2270-9
    1. Radio programs for children--United States--History.
2. Radio and children--United States. I. Title.
PN1991.8.C45B64   1989
791.45' 083--dc20   89-24133

To Danielle, Jamie, "Bubba," and Bailey

CONTENTS

PREFACE AND ACKNOWLEDGMENTS

Television began replacing radio as the daily source of entertainment for American children over forty years ago, but those who were still youngsters in the 1930's, 1940's and even into the 1950's haven't forgotten Jack Armstrong, the Lone Ranger, Terry Lee, Captain Midnight, Superman, and the other radio heroes they spent time with on a daily basis. As one of those "radio kids," I remember hurrying in to the living room to listen to "my programs," and sitting on the floor with my homework, ready to find out who the Lone Ranger would rescue next. Forty years from now, my grandchildren (to whom this book is dedicated) will no doubt remember *Sesame Street, Pee-wee's Playhouse, The Smurfs,* and *Garfield* with some fondness. The purpose behind *The Children's Hour* is to give the opportunity to find out what the children's radio programs were really like to those who never heard them.

There are, however, still sources for tapes of some of these shows. An excellent source of radio shows is the Broadcast Audio History Collection at Memphis State University, and this is where I obtained the majority of the tapes described in this book. Dr. Marvin Bensman, Director of these archives, also wrote an article entitled "Obtaining Old Radio Programs: A List of Sources for Research and Teaching," printed in *Journal of Popular Culture, 12,* Summer 1979, pp. 360-367. I owe a debt of gratitude to Dr. Bensman for his help. Other sources include Radio Yesteryear, Croton-on-Hudson, New York, and many private collectors.

The background material about the programs came from a variety of sources (besides my own memory):

magazine articles from the radio era, John Dunning's *Tune In Yesterday,* Jim Harmon's *The Great Radio Heroes,* Dick Osgood's *Wyxie Wonderland: An Unauthorized 50-Year Diary of WXYZ, Detroit* (birthplace of *The Lone Ranger*), Vincent Terrace's books, the *Complete Encyclopedia of Television Programs* and *Radio's Golden Years: The Encyclopedia of Radio Programs,* Raymond William Stedman's *The Serials,* and J. Frank MacDonald's *Don't Touch That Dial!* All of these books are fascinating reading for radio nostalgia fans as well as broadcast historians. An invaluable source of program listings and dates is Harrison B. Summers' *Thirty-year History of Radio Programs, 1926-1956.* Program dates were checked and cross-checked with all of these sources to provide as much accuracy as humanly possible.

Besides these excellent sources of program information, other books which will give readers an insight into the radio era are Hadley Cantril and Gordon Allport's *The Psychology of Radio,* Azriel Eisenberg's *Children and Radio Programs* (a study of New York children), Lawrence Lichty and Malachi Topping's compilation of material in *American Broadcasting: A Source Book on the History of Radio and Television,* John Houseman's *Run-Through,* and Christopher Sterling and John Kittross's *Stay Tuned: A Concise History of American Broadcasting.*

This book uses an alphabetical listing of the programs described in Chapter 5, similar to that in Dunning's *Tune In Yesterday,* and programs are listed under their complete title, such as *Adventures of Superman,* rather than just *Superman.* The list of programs is as complete as possible; some are quite well known and others are rather obscure. The criterion for choosing the programs was as follows: they had to be carried on more than just a local basis for at least part of the run, either syndicated or network. For instance, WOR's *Uncle Don* was on Mutual for a short time, and was included as an example of the "Uncle" shows. Most local children's programs would have been too difficult to obtain. The programs also had to be designed primarily with children in mind, even though broadcast in evening time periods. *Hawk Larabee* is included in some descriptions as a juvenile show, but the content of the episode reviewed was hardly aimed at children (drinking and women of ill repute), so this show was not included. Hopefully, not too many readers will find their favorite program omitted.

This book began as a paper for a Broadcast History seminar in 1971 when I started graduate school at Texas Christian University. I continued researching radio programs of the "thriller drama" genre at the University of Southern California, and began putting together all the materials necessary for the book about five years ago. My thanks to all the people who have helped me along the way, my advisors at TCU and USC, and for the moral support and advice from my colleagues at the University of North Texas. Also my thanks to my family, especially my husband John, for "putting up with me" during the writing process.

Chapter 1

Introduction

The Children's Hour

Between the dark and the daylight,
There comes from each radio tower
A series of gentle broadcasts
That are known as the Children's Hour.

And the girls and the boys are gathered
To listen with bated breath
To educational programs
Of Murder and sudden Death.

Then the air is athrob with sirens,
As the ears of the Little Ones
Tune in to the soothing echoes
of "gats" and of Tommy Guns.

And the eyes of the kids are popping
As they listen and wait, perplexed
By the educational problem
Of who will be rubbed out next.

Grave Alice and Laughing Allegra
And Harry and Dick and Tom
Hear music of sawed-off shotguns,
Accompanied by a bomb;

And quiver and shake and shiver
At the tender and pleasant quirks
Of a gang of affable yeggmen
Giving some "punk" the works!

And they listen in awesome silence
To the talk of some mobster group,
As they're opening up a bank vault
With nitroglycerine "soup."

Oh, sweet is the noise of battle
To children's listening ears,
As the guns of detectives answer
The guns of the racketeers;

And these educational programs
Will make the youngsters cower,
And the night will be filled with nightmares
Induced by the Children's Hour!

(Braley, 1937, p. 42).

In the early thirties, and encompassing a time span of over 20 years, the phenomenon which came to be known as "The Children's Hour" took over the radio network airwaves each evening from approximately 5:00 until 6:00 PM (including the surrounding time periods as well), inspiring Berton Braley's 1937 parody of Longfellow's poem. Children who never knew what time it was when such things as meals or homework were involved would appear as if led by some invisible Pied Piper for the Children's Hour. Often sitting on the floor in front of the radio set, just as children gather around the TV today, they were treated to a daily diet of mostly what parents termed "blood and thunder," although other tamer shows were also scheduled in the afternoons and on Saturdays. An *American Mercury* article in 1938 described what the children heard: "They listen for that first earsplitting sound which indicates that the Children's Hour is at hand. This introductory signal may be the wail of a police siren, the rattle of a machine gun, the explosion of a hand grenade, the shriek of a dying woman, the bark of a gangster's pistol, or the groan of a soul in purgatory" (Gibson, 1938, p. 294).

The   development   of   children's   television

programming was closely tied to the radio programs of the 1930's. Some of the well-known characters from radio, including *Superman* and the *Lone Ranger*, made their way directly to the small screen in the early 1950's. As children's television programming settled in to the Saturday morning time slot, cartoon characters as well as real-life characters were involved in the kind of mayhem that started on the Children's Hour. The *Violence Profile* of television programming compiled yearly since 1969, has shown the Saturday morning children's programs to be among the most violent on television (Gerbner, Gross, Signorielli, et al., 1979). The similarities in program content led to equally striking similarities in both the level and type of parental protest about the program content of much of the Children's Hour and the protests of parents about television programming for children. Articles appeared month after month in periodicals such as *Parents Magazine* informing of the dangers of listening to the children's radio programs. A 1933 *Parents Magazine* article said the programs were ". . . over-stimulating, often terrifying, producing bad after-effects of sleeplessness, fright, and nervous symptoms in children" (Littledale, 1933, p. 13). One horrified parent was quoted by *Scribner's Magazine* in 1933: "I have listened carefully, and I can say without fear of contradiction that every form of crime known to man is either committed or suggested in the majority of juvenile programs on the radio today" (Mann, 1933, p. 313). If these articles were reprinted today with the word "radio" changed to "television," few would notice the difference.

The program type which had become known as "thriller dramas" (analogous to television's "action adventure" programs) was the object of the parents' ire. The majority of these shows were serials, a form that made

its way into radio from comics and movies. What is
generally accepted as the first serial, *What Happened to
Mary*, appeared in the magazine *Ladies' World* in 1912,
and was soon made into a film. The first movie serials
were aimed at adults, but by the early 1920's, adult interest
was diminishing, and the serials became the domain of
children (Stedman, 1971). The serial form, distinguished
by "cliffhanger" endings, showed up on radio in 1931, with
the arrival of *Little Orphan Annie*; the character and title
borrowed from the comic strip. Others soon followed,
some from the comics, others from movies or books, and
still others originating on radio. Most of the serials
broadcast during the Children's Hour time slot were 15
minutes, running three or five times a week and using the
prerequisite cliffhanger ending at the close of each day's
program to entice the children to listen the next day. Most
of these shows were consistently sponsored and frequently
offered premiums that the young listeners could send away
for, accompanied by the inevitable box top.

    Although the serials commanded the attention of
those parents who objected to children's programs, there
were other types of programming for children, including
storytelling and the "Uncle" shows. Most of the
storytelling programs were run on Saturday mornings and
in the early afternoon, while the late afternoon Children's
Hour was dominated by the serial "thrillers."

    Music was the most typical type of programming in
the very early years. For example, in February, 1927, 74
percent of programming on New York City stations was
devoted to music, while slightly over one percent was
programming for children (Lundberg, 1975). The earliest
children's programs were mostly storytelling, and were
often run on a sustaining basis by the networks. Probably
the first radio drama for children was a play called *The*

Magic Journey, broadcast in 1923 on WLW (Lichty, 1975, p. 319). By 1932, children's programs made up 3.5 percent of total programming on nine major market stations. During the 1930's, the "thriller drama" increased steadily in importance in evening programming, as well as during the daytime. There was a high of 95 quarter-hours per week on the networks in the evening hours during 1951, and a high of 50 quarter-hours during the daytime in 1946 (Sterling & Kittross, 1978, pp. 520-521). The number of radio homes increased steadily from 12 million in 1930, to 23 million in 1935, and then to 30 million by 1940 (R. E. Summers & H. B. Summers, 1966).

The "thriller dramas" were quite popular with the young listeners, but some of their parents had high hopes of driving the radio "bogies" from the air. Children's programming expert Dorothy Gordon called for more educational programs presented in a manner the children would enjoy, with excitement and suspense. One program mentioned by Gordon (1942) was *Wilderness Road*, a dramatic serial of American frontier life, which won an award for best children's program given by the Women's National Radio Committee in 1936. *Wilderness Road* was off the air by 1937. Programs of this type, awards or no, were notoriously short-lived on radio, while the *Lone Ranger* rode on and *Superman* leaped tall building (in a single bound). Joseph Turow (1981), in his book *Entertainment, Education and the Hard Sell: Three Decades of Network Children's Television*, pointed out that the radio programs typical of the Children's Hour established a pattern for children's programming that carried over into television. That pattern was adventure programming with a law and order theme as the primary program fare for children. This has been the type of programming targeted by parents' groups, first in the radio years of the Children's Hour, and later on Saturday morning television.

Chapter 2

Popularity vs. Protest

The efforts made by parents' organizations to clean up children's programming have not been particularly successful. The pattern has been one of escalating violence, followed by increasing levels of objections, resulting in lesser amounts of mayhem, which appeased the protesting groups, for a time. Then the objectionable content would increase, and the cycle would start all over again.

The first radio serial thriller for children (*Little Orphan Annie*) came on the air in 1931, and within two years articles began appearing in various publications about the young listeners and their program preferences. One of the first studies was done in 1933 by the Child Study Association. Their survey made no pretense of being a statistical report, merely revealing trends shown by the results of a questionnaire answered by 80 women, mothers of a total of 134 children ranging in age from 2 to 15. The mothers reported their children enjoyed the radio, with ages from 10 to 13 having the greatest interest. Most of the children spent only 15 to 30 minutes a day listening, but 43 of them listened from one to three hours daily, and one boy of 13 listened for five hours daily. Most of the children preferred continued dramatic sketches and comedy programs ("Radio for children," 1933).

The Child Study Association also reported on a survey of 286 children in Scarsdale, New York, conducted by the Parent Teacher Association. These children ranged from third grade to seventh grade, and estimated the average time spent listening was eleven and one-half hours

per week, with the fifth and sixth graders reporting over 15
hours of weekly listening. The program most listened to
by the children was *Chandu the Magician,* with *Skippy*
second, *Little Orphan Annie* fourth, and *Buck Rogers*
fifth. Others listed included *Uncle Don, Bobby Benson,*
and *The Singing Lady.* The program list arranged by
enjoyment presented an unexplained discrepancy in what
the children listened to and what they liked. For example,
while *Buck Rogers* was second in liking and *Chandu*
third, *Little Orphan Annie* dropped to eleventh, *Skippy*
to 27th, and *Uncle Don* and *The Singing Lady* didn't
even rank in the top 40 programs rated for enjoyment.
Parents also rated these programs; only *Buck Rogers*
received a "good" rating, the other adventure programs
were rated "poor" to "very poor." When asked what type
program they wanted, almost half (47 percent) of the
children preferred "thrillers." One child went so far as to
request a "blood curtle murder" ("Radio for children,"
1933, p. 214.) A review of the Scarsdale study also
appeared in *The Nation* magazine in their April 5, 1933,
issue. "Poor and very poor programs will continue to
blight the homes of Scarsdale and of all America. For
children always win. Parents must take what comfort they
can in the contemplation of a revenge that is neither sweet
nor swift. It is to be found only in the probability that the
children themselves will some day be parents" ("The
children's hour," 1933, p. 362). Prophetic words, indeed,
with most of those children now grandparents, some of
whom no doubt complained about both the radio listening
and television viewing of their children; just as the current
generation of parents now complains about television fare
for the children of the 1980's.

Probably the most comprehensive study of children
and radio was Azriel Eisenberg's *Children and Radio*

Programs: A Study of More Than Three Thousand Children in the New York Metropolitan Area. Published in 1936, the book covered all aspects of listening behavior. Eisenberg found that children listened to an average of more than six hours per week, and among the programs they liked best were *Buck Rogers, Bobby Benson, Little Orphan Annie, Jack Armstrong, Skippy, The Lone Ranger, Let's Pretend,* and *Tom Mix.* These choices were interspersed with adult programs. The top choice of program type was "dramatizations" and almost a third of the children gave reasons for liking programs that were related to the content of the "thrillers"; *Buck Rogers* was considered the most exciting program. Eisenberg also studied the reactions to the programs. He found that 27 percent of the children reported lying awake at night thinking about programs they had heard, and 43 percent said they dreamed about programs. Of these dreams, 72 percent were unpleasant. The children were asked if they thought listening to the radio made them do "bad things," and 11 percent answered "yes." These undesirable behaviors learned from radio included stealing, disobedience, mischievousness, and playing with guns. Over a fifth of the children had written a letter to a program star, mostly to request some type of premium that had been offered. The respondents' parents were also questioned, and over 1500 of them listed benefits they thought their children had gained from listening, mostly concerning increased knowledge. However, 942 parents had banned certain programs, mostly the "thriller" type.

To say some parents reacted with dismay to the children's serials is putting it mildly. A *National Education Association Journal* article said home had become a nightmare and children were nervous wrecks, oblivious to everything else. And worse, they were taught to argue with their parents. "If your father and mother tell you that you must eat warm breakfast food to keep your bodies warm just tell them that they don't shovel hot coals on the fire to keep the house warm," was one advertiser's plea to sell cereal (Henry, 1935, p. 146). *Newsweek* in 1934 commented that children were easy prey for advertisers with the free premiums offered for box tops or package wrappers. The Child Study Association chairwoman was quoted as saying, "Radio seems to find parents more helpless than did the funnies" ("Protest," 1934, p. 27). Another parent observed that it was interesting to note that some of the programs parents considered the worst were the ones the children liked the best ("Mothers fighting," 1933, p. 32). A survey by *The Ladies Home Journal* of what the women of America thought about entertainment found 63 percent of the women thought some of the programs were too exciting for children. Furthermore, 57 percent believed it was the responsibility of the radio stations to keep these programs off the air (Cookman, 1939). One of the more drastic ideas came from an *American Mercury* writer: "Throw the radio set out the window" (Gibson, 1938, p. 296).

The various organized efforts against the programs began very early. A result of the before mentioned Scarsdale survey was a Parent Teacher Association movement in 1933 for less blood-curdling programs. Possible sponsor boycotts were suggested, and the Michigan Child Study Association sent the following petition to the sponsors of *Little Orphan Annie:* "We, the undersigned, hereby protest the broadcasting of the radio program Little Orphan Annie on the grounds that it is unwholesome entertainment for children, is over-stimulating and places too much emphasis on crime" (Mann, 1934, p. 246).

These several years of isolated protest had little effect, but by 1938 the protests had gained momentum and the networks responded with statements of policy regarding children's programming resulting from this pressure. NBC had published a code in 1934, and CBS had issued its "Statement of Policies" in 1935. The Women's National Radio Committee was formed in 1934, and Dorothy Gordon (1942) gave them credit for the portion of the CBS code relating to children's programming. Gordon listed the specific themes and treatments of drama which CBS said were not to be permitted in children's programming.

> The exalting, as modern heroes, of gangsters, criminals, and racketeers will not be allowed. Disrespect for either parental or other proper authority must not be glorified or encouraged. Cruelty, greed and selfishness must not be presented as worthy motivations. Programs that arouse harmful nervous reactions in the child must not be presented. Conceit, smugness, or an unwarranted sense of superiority over others less fortunate may not be presented as laudable. Recklessness and abandon must not be falsely identified with a healthy spirit of adventure. Unfair exploitation of others for personal gain must not be made praiseworthy. Dishonesty and deceit are not to be made appealing or attractive to the child (Gordon, 1942, p. 53).

CBS planned to create children's entertainment at a higher standard aimed at sound character development. The network hired a child psychologist to ensure that the programs met the approval of parents, teachers and the children. The NBC code, revised in 1939, became more specific concerning children's programs.

>All stories must reflect respect for law and
>order, adult authority, good morals and clean
>living. The hero and heroine, and other sympathetic
>characters, must be portrayed as intelligent and
>morally courageous. The theme must stress the
>importance of mutual respect of one man for
>another, and should emphasize the desirability of
>fair play and honorable behavior. Cowardice,
>malice, deceit, selfishness and disrespect for law
>must be avoided in the delineation of any character
>presented in the light of a hero to the child listener
>(MacDonald, 1979, p. 45).

But these efforts by CBS and NBC didn't keep the "thrillers" off the air. In April of 1947, *The Nation* reported that, while NBC and CBS had gotten rid of the serials, ABC and Mutual had nine "thriller" serials a day between them, broadcast at the same time, all with a blood and terror theme, and trying to outdo each other by "piling horror on horror in order to get the audience" (Frankel, 1947, p. 481). The National Association of Broadcasters had adopted a Code of Ethics in 1928, which was revised and expanded in 1935 and again in 1939. The code stated ". . .that the programs should reflect respect for parents, adult authority, law and order, clean living, high morals, fair play and honorable behavior. Such programs must not contain sequences involving horror or torture or use of the supernatural or superstitious or any other material which might reasonably be regarded as likely to overstimulate the child listener, or be prejudicial to sound character development" (H. B. Summers , 1939. p. 148).

The FCC had taken a dim view of the thrillers. FCC Chairman Anning S. Prall was quoted in a 1935 issue of *Parents Magazine:*

> Radio is not entirely meeting its obligations with regard to the effect it is having on the child mind of America. In certain cases I am certain that it is having a deleterious effect because of some of the programs that are being presented. I refer to the blood-and-thunder programs. I am not condemning all programs, for I know many that are distinctly educational. But the radio people would do well to eliminate programs that arouse the imaginations of children to the point where they cannot eat or sleep. Good clean adventure programs can be made educational. The Federal Communications Commission has the power to maintain a general surveillance over radio stations and networks in the public interest, convenience, and necessity" (Benedict, 1935, p. 22).

A 1937 *Newsweek* article reported that FCC Commissioner George Henry Payne said he was swamped with the largest amount of mail he had ever received on a controversial subject, and he said the children's radio programs should be cleaned up ("Radio gore," 1937, p. 26). In 1939 Commissioners Eugene O. Sykes and Payne issued a memorandum setting forth 14 types of programs which might be the basis of punitive action. The list included "cliff-hanger" kid shows (H. B. Summers, 1939).

One of the tactics employed by parents' groups to clean up radio was sponsor boycotts. Chase (1942) wrote that advertisers had shied away from the shows containing murder and excitement. He attributed this to the United Parents Association, whose recommendations included good English, suspense with a conclusion, stimulating the imagination, but with a definite educational or entertainment value. These efforts continued throughout the 1930's, and as late as 1947, *Time* reported that a Mrs. George Hanowell had mounted a petition drive to clean up radio, and had secured 350,000 signatures in 44 states, giving broadcasters a case of "the jitters" ("The children's hour," 1947, p. 63). The National Association for Better Broadcasting was formed in 1949, and violent content was an important issue for the organization from the beginning.

Not all parents felt this way, however. Some listened to the shows along with their children, others merely tolerated the shows and the devotion of the young listeners to the serials. By the late 1940's, when the handwriting was on the wall signaling the end of radio's golden era, many parents had accepted the shows and saw some benefits in them. A 1945 *Better Homes and Gardens* article said that outstanding educators and psychologists had examined the radio serials, along with comic books and movies, and had found they didn't have such a bad effect on kids after all. In fact, teachers had reported that radio-listening created good listening habits and stimulated interest and curiosity. The article also reported that, by then, the Child Study Association had decided that the premiums offered by radio stirred children to activity and participation, both wholesome and desirable. They put the responsibility on the parents for such things as program-induced nightmares: "If he finds such programs disquieting, interest him in listening to something else" (Schultz, 1945, p. 23). Other writers pointed out the increased social consciousness brought about by the programs, and the fact that the shows allowed the kids to "live dangerously yet remain within the reassuring safety of home" (Frank, 1949, p. 15). After all, many parents saw

that the majority of the young listeners were remaining
relatively undamaged by the blood-and-thunder.

Chapter 3

The "Effects" of Listening to the Radio

Most people would find it difficult to imagine life without television, and (for those old enough) it's difficult to remember what it was like without television. But memory serves some of us well, and we can remember growing up with radio as the daily entertainment; hurrying home after school to listen to *Jack Armstrong, Captain Midnight, The Lone Ranger*--and evenings spent with parents in the living room, gathered around the radio, listening to *Jack Benny, The Shadow, Edgar Bergen and Charlie McCarthy*. There wasn't that much difference between those evenings at home and family evenings now, spent watching the current television favorites.

Starting somewhere in the early 1960's, media researchers became increasingly enamoured with "effects" research. Since then, literally thousands of studies have been done, trying to determine what effect television viewing has on society. Of course, the vast majority of these studies deal with televised violence. The 1971 report popularly known as *The Surgeon General's Report on Television and Social Behavior* concluded that television content contained considerable violence, and that the viewing of televised violence appeared to increase the likelihood of aggressive behavior. Since then, George Gerbner's television "Violence Index" shows only minor fluctuations from year to year in the amount of such violence, and other research done by his team shows that heavy television viewers have a distorted perception of "real life" that is patterned after what they see on TV. Other researchers believe that the socialization of children by television contributes to an increase in the tolerance for violent behavior (Lefkowitz & Huesmann, 1980). Children grow up believing that "violence is a way of American Life and therefore not to be taken seriously. Moreover, since media violence is much more vicious than that which children normally experience, real-life aggression appears bland by comparison" (Drabman & Thomas, 1980, p. 331).

Unfortunately, very little of this type of research exists linking radio violence with aggressive behavior in children. Of course television is "show AND tell." Marty Halperin of the Pacific Pioneer Broadcasters said radio was plenty violent--"but you didn't see how it was done. You might say you're going to stab someone, but you don't know exactly how to do it: but you see it on television and you say, 'Aha! So that's how it's done'" (personal communication, April, 1977). The "Violence Index" applied to a sample of radio "thrillers" showed an amazingly similar amount of violence in those shows and television action-adventure shows, both for adults and those designed for children (Boemer, 1984). True, radio couldn't show the violence, but the power of the imagination may have created far worse scenarios in the mind than is shown on the small screen. Stan Freberg's demonstration of radio as the art of the imagination has us seeing in our mind's eye a mountain of whipped cream being shoved into Lake Michigan, which has been drained and filled with hot chocolate. Planes drop a ten-ton maraschino cherry into the whipped cream, to the cheering of 10,000 extras. Freberg concludes this scenario by asking, "You want to try that on television?"

Indeed, sound effects were designed to provide as much realism to the productions as possible. John Houseman (1972) described the painstaking process in the production of Orson Welles' *Mercury Theatre of the Air*.

Houseman reminisced about the production of *A Tale of Two Cities:* ". . . several hours of precious studio time were spent on the decapitation of Sydney Carton--the severing of the head and its fall into the basket. Various solid objects were tried under a cleaver wielded by one of the best sound men in the business: a melon, a pillow, a coconut and a leg of lamb. Finally it was discovered that a cabbage gave just the right kind of scrunching resistance" (p. 367). Other graphic descriptions of sound effects can be found elsewhere. "One hears the thud of the lead pipe against the head of the victim as well as the resulting crashing of the skull and his blood-curdling shrieks for help and mercy" ("Radio crime programs," 1940, p. 222). Cantril and Allport (1935) wrote, "A distinctive advantage of radio is its ability to produce 'close-ups' of sound, extracting the last ounce of emotional quality from even the 'sounds of silence.' And when it comes to producing eerie and uncanny effects the radio has no rival" (p. 232).

Of course, the prime example of how radio affected its listening audience is the *War of the Worlds* panic. This remarkable media event has no parallel in the history of television, for a significant number of the listeners to Welles' broadcast believed it to be the end of the world. Houseman (1972) and the others involved in the production found it hard to believe how gullible the public was, but there were contributory factors, among them the world situation with the impending war and the tremendous popularity of radio; not to mention the manner in which the program was produced. Herzog (1975) interviewed listeners about the event, and drew some conclusions about the causes of the unprecedented panic: the public had developed a great deal of confidence in radio; the economic insecurities and the threat of war; the technical features of the show; and the fact that many tuned in late, thus missing the introduction.

There were a handful of researchers looking into the questions of radio and children, with several articles published in the 1930's. H. P. Longstaff (1936) surveyed children in an attempt to determine the effectiveness of the children's radio programs; and he surveyed mothers (1937) to find out their opinions of the shows. He found the programs were popular and effective in selling their products; and he also found the mothers thought many of the programs were "unsuitable." John DeBoer (1937) found that children spent 2 to 3 hours daily listening, and they preferred radio drama. He also analyzed children's emotional responses to radio (1939), and found that the children responded intensely to radio drama, covering an extremely wide diversity of types of situations. DeBoer concluded "blood and thunder" was certainly effective in gaining an emotional response, but not really necessary.

Cantril and Allport (1935) found facts, narrative and abstract material better understood and more interesting when heard over the radio than when read on a printed page. And, in 1941, *The New York Times* reported on two research studies covering children's reactions to radio crime. One of the studies claimed that children who didn't listen to the shows had fewer fears, and no extreme fears at all. But in the other study, the researchers concluded that the violent content acted as a safety valve ("Dr. M. I. Preston's report," p. 22).

Others pointed to anecdotal evidence of radio's effects. Frank Reller, Chief Probation Officer of the St. Louis Juvenile Court, listened regularly to *Gangbusters* to determine what sort of mischief St. Louis juveniles would be up to in the next week. Forty-six young lawbreakers in one week of April, 1940, admitted to Reller that they took their cues from *Gangbusters* ("Listen, flatfoot. . .," 1940, p. 48).

A review of several polls in *Public Opinion Quarterly* asking Americans about the causes of crime found some respondents blaming radio programs, then television for juvenile delinquency (Erskine, 1974). James Gilbert (1986) wrote in *A Cycle of Outrage* that, during Senate hearings on the causes of juvenile delinquency in the 1950's, a much repeated idea was that the mass media was coming between parent and child. He pointed out that this was hardly a new idea: dime novels as well as other forms of popular culture had been similarly blamed before, and Fredric Wertham's *Seduction of the Innocent,* published in 1954, had blamed comic books as well as other forms of mass culture for inciting children to commit criminal acts. During the Senate hearings, a questionnaire was sent to 2000 citizens requesting opinions about the causes of delinquency. About half of them placed some blame on comic books and movies, and 75 percent of the unsolicited letters the committee received showed concern about comics, movies, radio and television. The results of the hearing were this: the causes of juvenile delinquency were many, and, although the media wasn't "proved" to be responsible, the senators insisted there must be improvements in the media industries. Gilbert disagreed with a narrow view of causality linking behavior to the consumption of media culture. But, on the other hand, he believed culture has an occasional determining effect on individuals. He concluded that if violence is a staple in daily life and approved by society, then we and our children will see violence as an acceptable action. Frank Orme of the National Association for Better Broadcasting said, "Even innocuous westerns, *Roy Rogers* or *Gene Autry,*--you've got the hero who always wins because he's more powerful, and you've got the helpless society

and helpless people who have to turn everything over to
them to protect themselves" (personal communication,
May, 1978). Orme described a 1946 survey of
psychiatrists and psychologists conducted by the PTA's in
Southern California--about 95 percent of those surveyed
were of the opinion the violence on radio was doing a great
deal of harm to children in general.

Whatever role the mass media has played in the
increasing amount of violence in our society, radio must
take its place and accept its share of any blame, for radio
set the pattern, leading children (and adults) to accept
violent programming with plenty of action as the norm.
Did children during radio's golden age believe the
programs? Cantril and Allport (1935) described Andrew, a
typical middle-class American boy of eight. Andrew's
mother had to rearrange her schedule to accommodate
Andrew's listening. Andrew believed *Little Orphan
Annie* and *Skippy* were real, while the comic characters
were make-believe. Why? "Because you can hear the real
ones on the air." Andrew believed the sponsors when they
told him that the only way to keep the programs coming to
him was to persuade his mother to buy the product. But
Andrew's imagination was expanded, and he learned many
interesting and useful things. Andrew preferred the stories
over the radio to those told him by his parents. Cantril and
Allport firmly believed in radio as the art of the
imagination:

> All children seem to enjoy the provocative
> effects of sound, and the freedom it leaves them for
> their creative fantasies. Television will add little or
> nothing to children's enjoyment of radio. It will
> constrain their imagery and tend to displace their
> aesthetic creations with a literal-minded and
> relatively dull reality. *Because of radio* Andrew's

outlook upon the world will surely be less provincial than that of his forbears and he may succeed in feeling more at home than they upon a newly shrunken earth (p. 239).

Chapter 4

Life in the Radio Era

Radio was a form of entertainment undreamed of in the history of mankind. Movies, plays, books--none could match the universal draw of radio, which was truly "something new under the sun." In the early 1920's, radio was a novelty; a hobby for some. But by the 1930's with the beginning of the Great Depression, radio had come into its own, bringing free entertainment to those people who could no longer afford plays or movies. There was humor, culture, news, plays--some type of entertainment for everyone. As Eric Barnouw (1968) pointed out in *The Golden Web,* people would give up their furniture, but not their radios; the shows were the only bright spot in the day when everything else was bad.

Life was grim, indeed, for many American children and their parents in the 1930's. The beginning of the decade saw a paralyzed economy, with people joining the ranks of the unemployed in droves. Over four million were without jobs in 1930; by 1932 the number had swelled to over 12 million. This amounted to one-fifth of the labor force, and this wasn't counting the millions who "made do" with part-time work. An average weekly wage in manufacturing was $16.21 in 1932, and the average annual income of the American middle-class in 1935 was $1348.00 (Phillips, 1969). Included among the unemployed were many white-collar workers, some of whom took to the highways along with their blue-collar counterparts. They had gone from being homeowners to renters, then to the ultimate indignity of being evicted. By the fall of 1932, there were an estimated one million transients, one-fourth of them under 21 (Phillips, 1969). Adding to the problem was the drought in the Midwest, which became known as the "Dust Bowl." The topsoil, depleted by years of over-cultivation, literally blew away in huge dust storms and brought many farm families into destitution and migration toward California. Shanty towns, called "Hoovervilles," sprang up along the roadsides, and some families considered themselves fortunate to have even a tent for shelter. Others who were unemployed and homeless became hoboes, riding the rails in search of employment. Small town children fortunate enough to have a roof over their heads and food to eat became accustomed to the "tramps" who came to the back door, asking to do odd jobs in return for a meal which was eaten sitting on the back step. But those children who were on the road with their parents were lucky to have food. Many of the youngsters worked in the fields alongside their parents--unable to go to school because of being on the move, plus lacking clothes and shoes.

By the middle of 1933, there was a glimmer of hope. It was because of the new President, Franklin Delano Roosevelt and his "New Deal," which included the "alphabet agencies" formed to aid the economy and get people back to work. The NRA (National Recovery Administration) regulated wages and working hours; the PWA (Public Works Administration) provided jobs and stimulated business by financing projects for public use; the WPA (Works Progress Administration) provided jobs that were supposed to be in the person's own line of work. These included artists, composers, and writers; thus the U.S. government became a patron of the arts. The CCC (Civilian Conservation Corps) provided jobs doing reforestation and conservation for some 2.5 million young unemployed men. The HOLC (Home Owners Loan

Corporation) was created to refinance home mortgages for those facing foreclosure (Time-Life, 1969).

By the end of the decade, the worst of the Great Depression was over, but now Americans were worried by the threat of war. No one wanted war--isolationism was the foreign policy; but Hitler began to take over more of Europe; there was civil war in Spain; the Japanese were invading China. But in spite of the economy and the impending war, there were many new and wonderful things coming into the lives of American children and their parents.

At home, there were more electrical appliances. Food might have been kept in an icebox in 1930, but by 1939 electric refrigerators were more common. Mothers kept the kids' clothes clean with an electric washing machine. It may have still been equipped with a wringer, but at least she didn't have to turn it by hand. Some homes were being heated by forced air furnaces, eliminating the need to constantly feed the big coal furnace in the basement. The "floor furnace" was under a grate in the floor, and occasionally a child was branded with squares on whatever part of her anatomy happened to hit when she fell on it. Clothing for girls growing up in the thirties was more comfortable--after all, it was a scant 10 to 15 years before that women wore heavy skirts to their ankles. However, girls still wore dresses to school, and only tomboys wore slacks for play clothes. A child's daily diet had been enhanced by such items as cold cereals (Wheaties), and treats like Popsicles, Dixie Cups and Eskimo Pies.

Children whose parents survived the Depression relatively unscathed sometimes were partially cared for by a live-in maid--a teen-aged farm girl, whose parents sent her to town so that she could attend high school. The girl got room and board and a little spending money in return for chores such as cleaning, baby-sitting, ironing and cooking.

The major health concern for kids was polio--the dreaded "infantile paralysis" with the majority of victims children. Many died; even more wound up crippled during the epidemics which occurred in the late summer and early fall. At the first hint of an outbreak, swimming pools closed, movie theaters were off limits to kids as were other public gatherings; sometimes the opening of school in the fall was delayed.

The automobile was well on its way to becoming a necessity. By 1935 there were 22 million motor vehicles, and every other family owned a car, even though it might have been somewhat dilapidated. The prices for new cars were fairly low, even by Depression standards--a Chevrolet business coupe was priced at $465.00 (Phillips, 1969).

Aviation was really coming into its own during the thirties, and children were fascinated by airplanes of all kinds, as well as the exploits of fliers like Charles Lindbergh, Wiley Post and Amelia Earhart. Commercial air travel was still somewhat of a novelty, but the maiden flight of the *China Clipper* in November, 1935 proved that trans-oceanic air travel was possible. It flew from San Francisco to Manila in 59 hours, 48 minutes, while a trip to Japan by boat took 15 days (Phillips, 1969). This interest in flying was reflected in the radio programs, with a number of them featuring an aviation theme, or at least including an airplane somewhere in the plot.

Other heroes of the thirties were those fighting crime--especially detectives and the "G-Men" of the FBI, who were dedicated to capturing the infamous crooks of the decade. These included John Dillinger, "Baby Face"

Nelson, "Machine Gun" Kelly and his wife Kate, "Pretty Boy" Floyd, "Ma" Barker and her four sons, and Bonnie and Clyde. There again, solving crimes and capturing the lawbreakers were major themes of the children's radio programs.

Although social consciousness in America was beginning to stir, prejudices of all kinds flourished and there was little, if any, social stigma attached to admitting these prejudices. Children of white, Anglo-Saxon, Protestant parents were often not permitted to play with kids who were "different," and this was certainly not restricted to blacks. Included were Jews, Mexican Americans, and any child with a last name that hinted of ancestors from a predominately Roman Catholic country. Girls were still excluded from many career fields; they were expected to learn "domestic science" from their mothers, so that they could become efficient housewives. Although more women were holding jobs, the "working mother" was a rarity.

Even at the height of the Depression, there were plenty of things for kids to do for entertainment. Radio, of course, held the top spot because it was free. Going to the movies was always a big treat, and children spent all Saturday afternoon at the local theater, watching a feature and an episode of the current serial that kept them coming back every week. Many of the serial heroes were also heard on the radio, with some of them going from movie serial to radio series; others from radio to the movies. The movie "musical" was a favorite with children, who were sometimes lucky enough to get singing lessons or dancing lessons, in the hopes they could become another Fred Astaire or Ginger Rogers, a Nelson Eddy or a Jeanette MacDonald; or even a Shirley Temple. Other kids' favorites were the *Andy Hardy* movies, *Blondie*, the

Dead End Kids, and the Marx Brothers. The thirties brought lucky young moviegoers two timeless classics: *The Wizard of Oz* and Walt Disney's first feature-length animated film, *Snow White and the Seven Dwarfs.* Children's favorite reading material was the "funnies," with a considerable number of comic strip heroes heard over the radio. Magazines were read by nearly everyone, and the youngsters were no exception. Besides those designed with the kids in mind, such as *Children's Activities,* older children liked *Life* and *Look* (all pictures); and *The Saturday Evening Post..*

There were at least a few news stories besides the captures of crooks that might have been interesting to children: the birth of the Dionne quintuplets (imagine having five sisters all at one time!); the kidnapping of the Lindbergh baby; the fall of the dirigible *Akron* and the *Hindenburg* explosion; King Edward's abdication of the throne to marry an American; the death of football coach Knute Rockne in a plane crash; the assassination of Huey Long, Louisiana's colorful governor.

Other interests of children included popular music--the era of the big bands had arrived, and radio brought the latest hits to every home, including songs with nonsense words that appealed immensely to young listeners--"Three Little Fishies," "Tutti Frutti," and "The Flat Foot Floogee." Baseball was the favorite sport of the decade, and baseball players were among the kids' heroes. Children played the game, too, as well as the newer game of softball. A big treat was a trip to the soda fountain at the corner drugstore, where a child could have a malt or an ice cream soda; a cherry or lime phosphate (a drink that has since disappeared); or a Coke flavored with any syrup (or combination of syrups) they had on hand. Children who lived in or near Chicago in 1933, or New York in

1939, had a real treat in store--a trip to one of the World's Fairs. Kids' favorite toys were still dolls and toy guns, but now they were often tied in with a child's hero from the movies, the comics, or radio. There were Shirley Temple dolls of all sizes, Dick Tracy wristwatches, Buck Rogers disintegrator guns, Tom Mix six-shooters, Little Orphan Annie rings and bracelets; not to mention the badges, whistles, and secret codes that could be obtained from the Children's Hour programs with a box top. All these diversions helped the youngsters and their parents live through the Great Depression; and gave little kids a legion of heroes and heroines to emulate.

The next decade of the Golden Age of Radio saw many changes for those growing up. The economy had improved, people were working; but the forties had hardly gotten underway when war came to the United States with the attack on Pearl Harbor. Everyone was expected to do his or her part for the war effort--even the children. Many of them saw their fathers go off to fight the Axis; those fathers who were either 4-F or too old for the service sometimes held down two jobs--a regular day-time job, and a night job at some type of defense plant. Mothers held defense jobs, too, as the country went all-out in the production of planes, ships, tanks and weapons. Even adolescents held down jobs after school--sometimes a teen-age boy was the oldest able-bodied male available. Kids gathered scrap for drives to collect metal, rubber and paper. Classes in school participated in these projects, plus others designed to help the soldiers--baking cookies, knitting squares to be assembled into afghans, making fudge, writing letters. The youngsters saved their pennies and bought War Stamps and Bonds.

Everyone had to give up some things: some foods were rationed, and so was gasoline. Those who had a small plot of land available had "Victory" gardens in which to grow their own vegetables. Other items had names with the prefix "Victory" attached. Children had to give up their balloon-tired bicycles (rubber was scarce) and ride skinny-tired "Victory" bikes. The family car (which was now considered pretty much of a necessity) was likely to be of 1930's vintage, for no American cars were manufactured from 1942 until after the war. Fathers became experts in patching up the car to keep it running throughout the war.

The middle of the decade, 1945, was singularly eventful, for this was the year the war finally ended--and President Roosevelt died, shortly after having been inaugurated for the fourth time. FDR had been President as long as most children could remember.

The post-war period, which coincided with the decline of radio as the foremost entertainment medium, brought prosperity to many families. There were still shortages--rationing of most foods lasted into 1946, and some until 1947. Meat was in short supply even into the 1950's. Detroit couldn't keep up with the demand for cars, even though there were 40 million of them on the road in 1948--enough for 30,000 Americans to die in traffic accidents that same year (Gunther & Quint, 1956). As the automobile became more important to families, it also became more important to kids, who dreamed of having their own "jalopies" when they became teen-agers. Whole families went with Dad to college on the GI Bill, which created a large population of married students and their children. Suburbs with huge housing developments sprang up almost overnight, and owning a home came within the reach of almost every family. With suburban living came even more gadgets--power mowers, automatic washing machines and clothes dryers, automatic dishwashers, and the barbecue pit. These devices provided more leisure time for everybody, especially mothers who were now looking for ways to use this time. Some found jobs; others joined clubs--bridge clubs, music clubs, service clubs. Women and girls were back to long skirts, with the "New Look," straight from Paris after the war. They were also giving themselves home permanents ("Which twin has the Toni?"), and girls of all ages were going to slumber parties. This was the beginning of the "bobby-soxer," and boys and girls alike wore jeans, white socks, penny-loafers, and Dad's white shirts with the shirt-tails out.

American children were healthier than ever before. The sulfa drugs and penicillin had made many serious childhood infections easily cured. The mastoiditis operation made necessary by ear infections, once commonplace, became virtually non-existent (Gunther & Quint, 1956). By the end of the Radio Era, polio had been conquered by the development of the Salk vaccine.

The early 1950's brought more war, with children once again seeing their fathers go off to fight--this time, the Communists in Korea. In spite of prosperity, this was a rather worrisome time for families. Communism, the H-bomb, flying saucers--all were subjects of discussion at home. Another worry was inflation: food that cost $5.00 in 1939 cost $11.97 in 1951; and then there was the ultimate worry of any child--their parents' divorcing. By 1954 one of 3.8 marriages failed (Gunther & Quint, 1956).

America's social consciousness was gaining ground--slowly at first, with the first black major league baseball player (Jackie Robinson) in 1945; the first black student in the previously all-white University of Arkansas Medical School in 1949 (Time-Life, 1969); culminating with the 1954 Supreme Court decision banning segregation in the public schools.

Throughout the forties and fifties, there were still plenty of diversions to entertain kids. During the war, cops-and-robbers and cowboys-and-Indians gave way to soldiers-and-Japs (or Nazis); the comic strip heroes went to war as soldiers or pilots; most of the radio heroes now fought spies rather than criminals, and some began to travel to exotic locations to fight the enemy. The youngsters still went to the Saturday matinees; the songs they sang were often tied to a war theme ("Praise the Lord, and Pass the Ammunition," "Der Fuehrer's Face," and "This Is the Army, Mister Jones"). A favorite of kids in the forties was another "nonsense" song, "Mairzy Doats." The middle forties saw the rise of the first real "heart-throb," Frank Sinatra, who had girls of all ages "swooning" over him and his songs. With the increase in cars came the drive-in movie--and the drive-in hamburger stand, which became favorite places to go for most children and adolescents.

But the post-war era brought another entertainment medium--television. The early development of TV was halted by the war: in 1945, there were six television stations on the air; by 1949, 98 television stations were broadcasting, and TV sets were being sold at the rate of 100,000 a week by the end that year (Gunther & Quint, 1956). This was the end of the Children's Hour, with the young listeners now becoming viewers by the thousands, watching *Hopalong Cassidy* and other radio heroes who could now be seen, plus *Howdy Doody* and *Kukla, Fran and Ollie* for the new generation of pre-schoolers. The Children's Hour programs didn't disappear until the middle 1950's, after the freeze on new television station construction permits had ended and virtually the entire country had access to viewing. The children's radio programs, however violent they might have been, reflected a less complex society than that faced by the latest generation of young television viewers. Life was simpler in some ways; values were more clearly black and white. Patriotism and national pride were a part of everyone's life; crime was always punished on the radio, and the "crime does not pay" message was backed by death for the criminal in many instances. The lawbreaker was often shot down by the cop, with no worry of whether or not he would have to face a panel of inquiry on the use of deadly force; or the criminal was executed, with no arguments about the morality of capital punishment. Regardless of the amount of crime and gore, the "thrillers" of the Children's Hour had one thing in common--the "good guys" were always good, and the "bad guys" were bad, and everyone knew the difference. Sometimes television blurs that distinction.

Chapter 5

The Programs of the Children's Hour--and Others

An overwhelming majority of the radio programs for children were of the "thriller drama variety". Out of 47 programs, only 9 were not classified as "thrillers." The programs described in this chapter fall into six general categories:

1. The Adventuresome Schoolboys (and girls). These included *The Adventures of Dick Cole, The Adventures of Frank Merriwell, Jack Armstrong, the All-American Boy, Little Orphan Annie,* and *Skippy.*

2. The Aviators and the Adventurers. These included *The Air Adventures of Jimmy Allen, Captain Midnight and the Secret Squadron, Don Winslow of the Navy, Hop Harrigan, Jungle Jim, Sky King, Smilin' Jack,* and *Terry and the Pirates.*

3. Superheroes and other Crimefighters. These included *The Adventures of Superman, Chandu the Magician, Dick Tracy,* and *The Green Hornet..*

4. Westerns. These included *Bobby Benson's Adventures, The Cisco Kid, Gene Autry's Melody Ranch, Hoofbeats, Hopalong Cassidy, The Lone Ranger, Mark Trail, Red Ryder, Renfrew of the Mounted, Rin Tin Tin, Roy Rogers, Sergeant Preston of the Yukon, Straight Arrow, Tennessee Jed, The Tom Mix Straightshooters, Wild Bill Hickok,* and *Wilderness Road.*

5. Space Adventurers of the Future. These included *Buck Rogers in the 25th Century, Flash Gordon, Space Patrol,* and *Tom Corbett, Space Cadet..*

6. Educational and Storytellers. These included *American School of the Air, The Cinnamon Bear, Dorothy*

Gordon, Let's Pretend, No School Today, Popeye, Uncle Don, The Singing Lady, and *Smilin' Ed McConnell and the Buster Brown Gang.*

The thrillers had several main plot themes; most dealt with crime, and criminals were plentiful, whether in the city or out on the range. There were mysteries with plots ranging from the mundane (missing class records) to danger for the hero (being held prisoner with the threat of death). During the war, most plots dealt in some way with enemy spies. There was plenty of violence, including cold-blooded murder and one suicide. The heroes (and others) were often rendered unconscious by a blow to the head, from which they recovered with no apparent ill effects. Locales were often exotic far-away places, or they were set in the West. Little distinction was drawn between the Old West and the West of modern days, in that the characters of both eras usually traveled by horseback and carried six-shooters.

Love and romance were not part of the plots--to include them was apparently the kiss of death for a show. Only three of the programs to be described, *Flash Gordon, Jungle Jim,* and *Smilin' Jack,* had romantic themes, and it should be noted none of them lasted even a year on the air. Romance was only hinted at in *Buck Rogers,* and in a way kids could relate to (the characters seemed embarrassed). *Little Orphan Annie* stands alone as the one female main character; other female roles were strictly secondary.

There were really obvious differences in style and production between the earliest shows and those of the late 1940's and the 1950's. The majority of the early programs were 15 minutes in length, and were usually serials. Those that were on the air toward the end of radio drama were mostly the 30-minute, complete-in-one-episode format. Productions became more "polished" as time passed, with more realistic sound effects and music bridges. The early programs relied on narration to explain the story line; later this was accomplished through dialogue. In the later shows, the actors' voices sounded "right" for the character--the heroes had deep, resonant voices; the villains sounded raspy and unpleasant. Voices also had to be representative of the characters' ages, and they had to be so distinctive that listeners could tell them apart. This was not always the case in the earliest examples.

The plots often had highly implausible elements, no matter when the shows were broadcast; but plots became more complex in the later programs, perhaps reflecting increased sophistication in the young listening audience. It seems probable that one of the most influential writers was Fran Striker, who wrote *The Lone Ranger,* as well as *The Green Hornet* and *Sergeant Preston.*

At least one episode of all but two of the programs is described. No tapes were located of *Skippy* or *Dorothy Gordon* shows. Whenever possible, there are two episodes described of programs that were on the air for a long period of time, or programs that had two or more runs. (If available, one episode was chosen from the early shows, and one from the later period.) The programs tended to be quite stable in content and characters, no matter how long they were on the air. The major differences were those mentioned before--the use of narration, sound effects, and attention to voice characterizations.

THE ADVENTURES OF DICK COLE

One of the shows with the adventuresome schoolboy theme, *The Adventures of Dick Cole,* lacked the action and the exotic locales of *Jack Armstrong,* but did bear some resemblance to *Frank Merriwell* (another of the schoolboys, in a turn-of the-century setting). Dick, like Frank, was a mature-sounding righteous lad, who solved the crimes that cropped up at his school, Farr Military Academy. If Dick and Frank's schools had been taken literally as examples of boarding schools, few parents would have sent their teenage boys to such places, where crime and gambling were rampant! The character came straight to radio as a syndicated show from the pages of *Blue Bolt Comics* in 1942, and the show's run was fairly short, probably lasting less than a year.

If the 1942 episode obtained was an example, it's easy to understand why the show was short-lived. First we hear the announcer: "Presenting Dick Cole and his thrilling adventures at Farr Military Academy!" Next is the theme song, presumbably sung by Dick and his cohorts,

> "We'll always be near to Farr,
> we'll praise her where'er we are;
> We'll praise her each day with a hip-hip-hooray;
> it's a rule there's no school like Farr!
> We'll sing out our loyalty!
> We'll ring out with voices free!
> As we travel through life, we will follow our star,
> we'll always be near to Farr!"

Returning, the announcer says, "Listen, boys and girls, today we bring you another exciting episode of *The Adventures of Dick Cole* at Farr Military Academy. You've known Dick Cole in *Blue Bolt Magazine* and in *Foremost Comics* for a long time, and now you meet him every week at this time over this same station on the air. In just a moment, you'll hear from Dick Cole himself; but first, here's a message you'll all want to hear." The theme music plays for a while, as background for a commercial to be inserted. "And now, here's Dick Cole, with a word about today's thrilling episode." Dick says, "Hi, gang! That word 'thrilling' about today's episode is really so. In any event, it seemed plenty thrilling to me, especially when I came within one or two minutes of being killed! Yes, and if I hadn't suspected a fellow cadet at Farr by the name of Pritchett of being a foreign spy, I wouldn't be here right now! And there were some people who turned out to be even more surprised about Pritchett than I was--and that was a mighty good thing, too. But, to begin the story at the beginning, we had some special field manuevers going on at Farr, with the cadet corps concentrating on artillery fire! (Sound effects: big guns firing) I was in charge of a special gun--a 105-millimeter howitzer. What was so special about that gun? Well, that's what my roommate Simba Carna, wanted to know when he came across the field." It turns out that the gun was special because of the range-finder that Major Farr has invented. Dick calls his gunner, Phil Pritchett, over and we find out that Dick is the only one privileged to know how the range-finder operates. Phil is curious and wants to know how it works, but the Major tells him it's top secret. It seems the Major is intending to offer the range-finder to Washington, and orders Dick and Simba to guard the gun overnight. When Dick goes to relieve Simba, he hears twigs snap and sees someone lurking in the bushes. Dick suspects Phil, and goes to Phil's tent, but Pritchett is asleep in his cot. He reports the incident to Major Farr, who tells Dick it was probably his imagination. Dick is on guard duty for a couple of hours, when suddenly two men jump him and knock him out! The spies take pictures of the range-finder, and they decide to take Dick with them in case he could identify them. When Dick comes to, he is bound and gagged in a strange house.

One of the men takes the gag out of Dick's mouth--"You're filthy spies, and you won't get away with it!" The spies tell Dick they are going to kill him, but he cleverly tells them that there is a part of the range-finder that has been removed for safe-keeping, and their pictures will do them no good. Dick tells them (in return for sparing his life) that only one person besides the Major knows about it--"another cadet at Farr named Phil Pritchett." The spies return to the Academy and kidnap Phil, bringing him to the hideout. Phil tells Dick he made so much noise it was a wonder the whole cadet corps didn't wake up. Dick says that's good, and tells Phil to stall for time. The spies threaten them with a box of torture instruments, and are about to take a knife to Phil, when the Major and the police arrive in the knick of time to arrest the spies. The spies ask how they knew where to find them--Major Farr says, "It wasn't I who outsmarted you--it was a boy named Dick Cole who outsmarted you!" One of the spies grumbles, "You see, tha-that's the big kid there--I told you he was bad luck for us!" It turns out that Dick knew the Major would be watching Phil because of Dick's suspicions and would follow the spies when they kidnapped Phil. Dick had used Phil as "bait!" The announcer returns to close with, "Be sure to listen in next week, Dick Cole fans, same time same station, for another exciting half-hour with Dick Cole at Farr Military Academy. Yes, meet Dick Cole every week on the air, and enjoy his thrilling radio adventures as you've enjoyed him and his life at Farr in those two favorite comic magazines, *Blue Bolt* and *Foremost Comics*. And now, here's Dick Cole." Dick says, "So long, gang, I'll be seeing you all next week, so remember to listen for us--it's a date!"

Implausible plot line, poor script, pretty bad acting--all no doubt contributed to the early demise of the series. Just as in the early *Frank Merriwell* episodes, the actor portraying Dick had a very mature-sounding voice for a military academy student, although Phil and Simba had younger-sounding voices. This episode had plenty of violence--kidnappings, threat of death, and torture, complete with a box of torture instruments, presumably too awful to be described, although the first one the spies selected was a knife. This was not terribly exotic, but surely enough for a nightmare or two. Dick, of course, was insufferably good, strong, clever and trustworthy.

THE ADVENTURES OF FRANK MERRIWELL

Another radio schoolboy hero who really got around was Frank Merriwell. Frank originated in the pages of some "dime novels" written by Burt L. Standish in the 1890's, then came to radio as a 15-minute three-times-a-week-serial in 1933. The earlier radio show went off the air sometime in the thirties, and came back to NBC in 1946 as a 30-minute show. There was a *Frank Merriwell* movie serial in 1936, which changed the story's setting to 1936. Jim Harmon (1972) wrote in *The Great Movie Serials* that Frank served as the inspiration for *Jack Armstrong* and observed that both had names that were plays on words. Frank (straighforward); Merry (sense of humor); and Well (physically fit) (pp. 80-81). Both characters were schoolboy heroes, and both were insufferably perfect. However, the setting for Frank was the turn of the century, so his adventures and athletic feats were limited to terra firma. The locale for the early stories is Frank's school, Fardale Academy, where Frank and his pal Bart Hodge are roommates.

The opening for the earlier series and the run in the

1940's differ considerably. The episode of August 7, 1933, begins with the sound of reveille. Announcer Harlow Wilcox intones, *"The Adventures of Frank Merriwell!* Tonight's episode--'Frank Confesses in the Dark.' (Sound effects: Bong----bong----bong). Three o'clock in the morning--that must be the time when Frank makes his confession. We don't have to wait that long to hear about it, however, because it's in tonight's episode. These adventures are brought to you three times a week by the makers of Dr. West's double-quick toothpaste." The commercial consists of a premium offer; "a live pet--a racing turtle only about an inch-and-a-half long." We must stay tuned to find out how we can acquire this little pet. A lot of the story is told in the beginning narrative: "Well, let's go back to Frank Merriwell's last adventure and see where we left him--in a bad spot, I'm afraid. You see, Frank has always been a model student at Fardale Academy, but the last time we left him playing poker with a bunch of cadets who call themselves the 'Black Sheep.' Now playing poker isn't a very healthy pastime for young military students, is it? But this is the way it happened--how Frank happened to get in with this crowd. Frank caught his roommate Bart Hodge sneaking out of their room sometime after taps, after they were supposed to be in bed. Bart wouldn't tell where he was going, so Frank insisted upon going along. They slipped down the hall to Hugh Bascombe's room--and much to Frank's surprise, a lively game of poker was going on. For a long time, Frank refused to join in. But finally, much to our surprise, he did, and he was lucky. He began to win right from the first. Hugh Bascombe was furious, because it seemed that *he* always managed to be the winner in previous games, and tonight he's a heavy loser. Hugh's friend Leslie Gage has no use for Frank either. Let's see now how the game stands. The final pot is the biggest of all, and the stiff betting has forced everybody but Hugh Bascombe, Bart Hodge and Frank Merriwell to withdraw from the game. It's Bascombe's turn to meet Frank's last raise." Finally, after all this build-up, we make it to the dialogue. Frank and Bart keep raising, until Hugh is forced out. He accuses them of ganging up on him, which they were (Frank is holding a pair of deuces). Frank also drops out, and Bart is left with the winnings. "I needed this to pay the mortgage on the old homestead." Frank gives Bart the few chips he has left. "I don't propose to take any money out of this room that isn't my own." Bart and Hugh begin to scuffle, and a knock on the door warns them they're making too much noise. Frank and Bart sneak back to their room, and Frank tells Bart of his suspicions about Hugh. "I watched him so close he couldn't make his luck work for him the way he usually does. He knew I was watching him so he didn't try any tricks. That's what made him so furious." Bart asks, "Do you think he cheats?" Frank replies, "Well, I wouldn't want to say so with no more proof than I have--but no honest player has luck at poker all the time." Then the long-awaited confession occurs. Frank wants to tell Bart something--something serious. "Sit down here, old man, and I'll confess to you, unburden my soul, reveal my shame--in the dark so you can't see me." It seems that gambling is Frank's weakness! Bart is astounded! "Now you admit you have a weakness! Why--why, gee, man, you--you're human!" Apparently Bart and Frank were never close pals until this moment. Frank further confesses that once he stole two dollars from his mother's purse to gamble, and lied to her when questioned about it. He later owned up to this sin, and was forgiven by his late mother, who had taught him his strong sense of right and wrong. A gambler, a thief and a liar! What next? After Frank's

mother died, he went back to gambling until he learned of
the death of his father, who had gone out West to seek his
fortune. Dad had been shot over a card game. Frank's
uncle told him about his father's gambling weakness. This
had caused Frank to swear off gambling--until this night.
Frank tells Bart he has understood Bart's behavior
sometimes better than Bart understands himself. Bart has
faith in Frank. "You'll never gamble again, Frank, I know
it, pal!" The announcer returns with, "Well, imagine Frank
being brave enough to make that confession to Bart Hodge,
the boy who had always disliked him so much! But I don't
think he dislikes him any more, do you? No, sir, I think the
air's all cleared between these two and from now on, they'll
really be pals. Pals--say, it's time to tell you about your
new pal, that tiny racing turtle!" He goes on to tell the
young listeners to send in the paper cartons from two large
size tubes of Dr. West's double-quick toothpaste to get the
turtle. "Mail them to Dr. West, in care of the station to
which you are listening." After further touting the virtues of
a pet turtle, he closes with, "Now--about Frank Merriwell's
next adventure. It's called---(Sound effects: crowd
cheering, and the sound of a bat hitting a ball)--'Frank Is
Knocked Out!' Remember to tune in on Friday and hear all
about how it happpened, how Frank is knocked out. *The
Adventures of Frank Merriwell* come to you every
Monday, Wednesday and Friday at this same time. This is
Harlow Wilcox speaking. So long." The show concludes
with the sound of reveille.

This early episode is very dated, and listening to it
makes it easy to understand why it didn't last. The voices
of the actors sound very mature to be students, and the
distinction between the voices is so slight that it's very
difficult to figure out who is talking. There wasn't much
action, and it's difficult to imagine even children of the

1930's being naive enough to be able to stomach such a "holier-than-thou" character.

By the second run, the program has been expanded to 30 minutes; the boys have graduated from Fardale, and are at Yale. One of the later episodes, broadcast October 23, 1948, has a different opening. (Sound effects: a trotting horse) The announcer's words: "There it is, an echo of the past, an exciting past, a romantic past--the era of the horse and carriage, gas-lit streets and free-for-all football games, the era of one of the most beloved figures in American fiction, Frank Merriwell. Merriwell is loved as much today as ever he was, and so the National Broadcasting Company brings him to radio, in a new series of stories based on the famous books written by Gilbert Patton under the pen name Burt L. Standish. Today, the Mystery of the Missing Records. It's the morning of the traditional Yale-Princeton football game, and the Yale campus is live with the excitement over the impending battle. As our story opens, Frank and Bart are crossing the quadrangle when they are greeted by Inza Burrage." The three discuss the game, and the new scholastic eligibility requirements for the players. Frank and Bart tell her they are on their way to see Johnny Lane, a transfer from Princeton who works in the registrar's office. He is gathering the scholastic records for Jeff Woodward, a Yale team member who is worried about his math grades. Johnny lives on the top floor of a hall next to the bell tower--"the cheapest room at the University." He tells them Jeff's grades are all right. Bill Hopkins comes in, and Johnny tells them he'll drop the records off--after he makes another stop. Later, Bill sees Johnny go to the home of Butler, a Princeton alumnus, and give him some papers, for which he is paid! Now Johnny can buy a new suit, which he does before delivering the records to Professor Forrest. He runs into the Dean at the Professor's office; the

Dean asks to see the records. But when the coach gets the eligibility list, Frank and Bart are not on it! They go to see the Professor, who says he didn't receive any of their records, even though their grades were excellent. Several of their instructors have gone out of town, so getting duplicates is impossible, and Johnny Lane is nowhere to be found! Frank and Bart must find him; meanwhile, the game begins without them. Bill and Inza talk at the game, and Bill figures out that Johnny Lane must have given the records to Butler. Frank and Bart go to Johnny's room, and Bill bursts in, accusing Johnny. Johnny denies it, saying their names were on the list. He refuses to tell what he gave Butler. Frank believes Johnny, because he has given his word. Back at the game, Princeton is leading, and the Dean asks Inza where Frank and Bart are--she tells them about the missing records, and the Dean realizes that he has them! He gives the records to Inza, who delivers them to the coach. Frank and Bart join the game, and they come from behind to win. They are all invited to lunch with the Dean, and Frank has found out that Butler, as a local business man, was supposed to give a talk to a Yale economics class. He didn't have time to prepare, so he had Johnny ghost-write it for him! The Dean says he owes an apology to the entire student body. The announcer closes with, "And so ends another exciting adventure with Frank Merriwell, the loved hero of American fiction, brought to you in a new series of stories by the National Broadcasting Company. And be sure to listen again next week at this same time when Frank Merriwell returns in another of his celebrated exploits. And now, here is Frank Merriwell himself, with some very distinguished guests." Frank tells about a four-year scholarship to the University of Denver, awarded by the National Youth Month Committee. He introduces the sponsors of the committee, which was designed to combat juvenile delinquency. They present the scholarship to the winner. The announcer gives the credits: "Frank is played by Lawson Zerbe, Bart by Harold Studer, Inza by Elaine Rost. Other members of the cast were Dick Keats, Arthur Maitland, Bob Dryden, Ivor Francis and Donald Duka. Original music is by Paul Taubman. *The Adventures of Frank Merriwell* is written by Ruth and Gilbert Braun and William Welch, and the entire production is under the direction of Jack Kuene. Listen again next week at this same time, 12:30 PM, over most of these NBC stations for *The Adventures of Frank Merriwell*. This is Mel Brandt speaking."

Although the voices of the actors in the later shows sound more like those of college students, the four younger male voices in this episode were very difficult to tell apart. The script and dialogue are somewhat more exciting than the earlier program, but the "holier-than-thou" theme is still very much a part of the story. At least there were no murders, and the only violence was a scuffle in the early episode. The second run ended in 1949.

THE ADVENTURES OF SUPERMAN

Of all the denizens of the Children's Hour, only the Man of Steel has retained his popularity into the 1980's. True, re-runs of other characters from radio who crossed the bridge into television are still being shown in some markets; but Superman is still a star, thanks to the *Superman* movies.

After first appearing in *Action Comics* in 1938, it was a relatively short leap for Superman to the airwaves. After an initial series of syndicated shows, *The Adventures of Superman* came to Mutual in 1940 as a 15-minute serial, three times weekly. Clayton "Bud" Collyer (later of TV's

To Tell the Truth) played Superman throughout most of the show's run, and Joan Alexander was Lois Lane. The show was dropped for a short time in 1942, but, because of its popularity with the children, returned as a Monday through Friday 15-minute serial. Kellogg's Pep began sponsoring Superman in 1943. Another series of leaps brought Superman to the Saturday afternoon movie serials in 1948, and later to television as a syndicated 30-minute show in 1953.

The Man of Steel wasn't quite impervious to the objections of the anti-blood and thunder group, however; and one mother objected because a neighbor's child had attempted to fly off the garage roof shouting "Up, up. . . and Away!" (Whiteside, 1947). Superman overcame the objections; first, by going to war and battling the enemy in 1943, and later, after the war, by battling bigotry and intolerance. The first attempt at injecting social consciousness into the show was described by *Newsweek* as a sequence involving Superman getting a bunch of young bigots to establish an Inter-Faith Community House. Also in the works were sequences on juvenile delinquency and school absenteeism ("The cereal hour," 1946). Racial intolerance was targeted, Ku Klux Klan code words were revealed by Superman, and the show acquired a new listener: one Samuel Green, Grand Dragon of the KKK, who reportedly had to listen in order to supply new code words to replace those given out over the air. A Kenyon and Eckhardt (Kellogg's advertising agency) executive said that parents' organizations were congratulating them on the show, and that the Hooper ratings had actually gone up since the social episodes were introduced (Whiteside, 1947). MacDonald (1979), in *Don't Touch That Dial!*, called *Superman* the most explicitly progressive series for children.

The December 8, 1944, episode began with the announcer: "Presenting--*The Adventures of Superman!*" Then the words that most kids had memorized open the show: *"The Adventures of Superman!* Faster than a speeding bullet! (Sound effects: gunshot sound) More powerful than a locomotive! (Sound effects: train sound) Able to leap tall buildings in a single bound! (Sound effects: Whoosh!) Look! Up in the sky! It's a bird--it's a plane--it's Superman! Yes, it's Superman, who is today trying to find Jimmy Olson. We'll join him as Clark Kent in a moment--but first. . ." He then told the kids how they could win a $25.00 War Bond. The listeners were to write to the program and tell what kind of adventures they preferred for Superman. "If you prefer to have Superman involved in a mystery story, tell us about it. If your preference runs to spy stories or adventures with saboteurs or gangsters, be frank with us." The children were urged to think back on the programs they had heard and tell which they liked best. The winning entry would win the War Bond. "And now, *The Adventures of Superman!* Suffering from complete loss of memory, Lois Lane is under the control of an enemy agent posing as her uncle. And as a result, a baffling mystery has developed for Superman and his friends. Telling Lois that Perry White and Clark Kent had stolen the plans of a new Allied secret weapon which they intended to sell to the Japs, and accuse her of being a saboteur, the bogus Uncle John induced her to remove a set of the plans from Editor White's safe. But while Lois was having dinner at a restaurant with Jimmy Olson, the plans disappeared from her handbag. Certain that Jimmy had taken them, Uncle John waylaid him and drove him away in his car. As we continue now, Superman, worried over Jimmy's absence, has arrived at Lois's apartment, and having resumed his guise as Clark Kent, is ringing the doorbell." Lois and Clark talk, and Lois is acting very strangely. The phone rings, and Lois pretends it's "Bob." Superman suspects it was really Uncle John, and, using his X-ray vision, was able to get Uncle John's phone number that Lois had written by the phone. Clark leaves, and becomes Superman. Meanwhile, the fake uncle has Jimmy tied in a chair in a shabby apartment over a garage. He threatens Jimmy with unnamed torture if he doesn't give Uncle John the plans, which had been given to White to publish when the War Department gives permission. Lois phones to tell Uncle John about Clark's visit, so he and Jimmy start to leave. Meanwhile, Clark Kent has gone to a detective friend, who had the phone number traced, giving him the address. Once more, Clark becomes Superman, and he goes to the rescue! The announcer closes with, "You're too late, Candy. Clark is on his way to the Parkside garage as Superman. Will he arrive in time to intercept the mysterious Uncle John and Jimmy Olson? And what has happened to the plans of the important secret weapon?" Fellows and girls, don't miss Monday's exciting episode in this fascinating new mystery story! Tune in same time, same station, for--*The Adventures of Superman!* Faster than a speeding bullet! (Sound effects: gunshot) More powerful than a locomotive! (Sound effects: train) Able to leap tall buildings in a single bound! (Sound effects: Whoosh!) Look! Up in the sky--it's a bird! It's a plane! It's Superman! (Sound effects: Whoosh!) Follow *The Adventures of Superman* every day, Monday through Friday, same time, same station. *Superman* is a copyrighted feature appearing in *Superman D.C. Publication.* This is Mutual."

Everything about the plot is far-fetched, perhaps more so than most of the other programs. Lois has a complete memory loss, but she knows who everyone is.

Why would a newspaper editor be given secret weapon plans to publish and be kept in his safe? And how would the bad guys know the plans were there? Of course, if the kids believed that Superman could fly through the air and had X-ray vision, these minor details likely made no difference.

Another Superman episode, from May 8, 1945, was sponsored by Kellogg's Pep, and was devoted to a war theme. It began with the same opening, followed by: "Yes, it's Superman, who is today completely mystified by the strange attack that seized Jimmy Olson and Tony Sloan at the Lair of the Dragon." This was followed by a plea for children to help their parents save scrap metal, etc., for the war effort in the Pacific, now that the war in Europe was over. The story line concerned a "Jap" called the "Dragon," who had a secret weapon capable of killing whole villages at one time. It began with Jimmy and Clark and *Daily Planet* war correspondent Tony Sloan having been captured by the Dragon. Suddenly, Jimmy and Tony declare that the flowers on the wallpaper are leaping out at them, and they conveniently lose consciousness long enough for Clark to turn into Superman and rescue them. He flies out the window and down to a park with them, and gives them artificial respiration--"Out goes the bad air, in comes the good air." Superman goes back to the house for the Dragon, but the house explodes before his eyes! He resumes his Clark Kent identity and returns to the park, where he tells Jimmy and Tony about the mysterious explosion and the Dragon's disappearance. Tony realizes their losing consciousness and the house's blowing up was because of the Dragon's secret weapon! Tony then relates the story of the Dragon's murder of the entire population of a South Pacific Island by the Dragon's "secret weapon." The plane Tony was in was shot down by the Japs, but he

survived in a life raft. He came upon a tiny island with
only one native on it. He was the only man in the world
who knew of the Dragon's secret weapon, and lived to tell
about it! In a flashback, we hear the native, Sing Song, tell
that the island had been large, with 3000 people on it. The
Japanese came and shot his father and others, then threw
bits of colored paper in a volcano and left. One hour after
the Japs had left, the people began to see flowers coming
out of the ground at them, and then the island blew up, and
everyone but Sing Song died. "Incredulously, Clark Kent
and Jimmy Olson stare at Tony Sloan, not knowing
whether to believe or disbelieve his shocking story." This
was followed by the standard closing.

This particular episode contained a lot of
description of violence in the flashback; most of it about
killing and how bad the Japs were. Both *Superman*
episodes followed the usual serial format, with just enough
action to maintain interest, and the cliffhanger ending. The
productions had plenty of sound effects, and good voice
characterizations. Superman's voice was deeper-sounding
when he changed from Clark Kent into the Man of Steel.
Superman moved to ABC in 1949, and left the radio in
1951.

THE AIR ADVENTURES OF JIMMY ALLEN

Flying was perhaps even more fascinating to
children in the 1930's and 1940's than it is now, and many
of the shows were built around an aviation theme. Even
those heroes not originally aviators (such as Jack
Armstrong) often became world air travelers. The first
pilot to appear on the Children's Hour was Jimmy Allen, a
sixteen-year-old who flew around solving crime and facing
danger with his sidekick and fellow pilot, Speed Robertson.

Jimmy was heard as a 15-minute serial from 1933 until around 1936; the original transcriptions were re-released in the early forties for another run (Dunning, 1976). The boy aviator was also featured in a 1936 film, *The Sky Parade*.

Episode number 1089, labeled as a 1935 broadcast, began with the music theme--it had a military flavor, and the tinny, scratchy sound of an old Victrola. The music segues into the sound of a small plane; and the announcer begins with: *"The Air Adventures of Jimmy Allen!"* The theme music comes up. The recording of the episode reviewed then featured a promo for the series in an attempt to gain sponsorship. "My time will be your time when you're on the air--time for your opening commercial announcement in which you tell your enthusiastic juvenile audience about yourself and your product." The announcer continued to extoll the virtues of sponsoring Jimmy Allen; it appears to be a recording used as a sales tool rather than for broadcast, probably during the later run. "This epic program was written by two World War I Aces, men who know their aviation from A to Z and who have national reputations as writers." (The writers were Robert M. Bartt and Wilfred G. Moore, who later wrote *Captain Midnight.)* After the promo, we return to the program. "Jimmy and Speed Robertson have incurred the hatred of the Benders, father and son. The boys have discovered the reason for Rip Bender's great desire to buy the Croft Ranch--the precious gold of the Chihuahua treasure, buried in the mountains of the Croft property. In the last episode, Rip Bender's scheme to do away with the boys took form, and he asssured his father that the plan would be successful. It is now early morning. Jimmy and Speed are about to take off to fly over the mountains in search for landmarks as shown on the map of the treasure. Flash Lewis is working around the airplane as the boys

approach." Flash tells them the plane is almost ready to go,
and wishes he could go along. Speed (who appears to run
things) says Flash needs to stay around, because he doesn't
want Mrs. Croft and Barbara left alone with "those
Benders running around." Speed tells Jimmy he plans to fly
over the mesa and circle the ranch house several times, so
Ortez will give them a signal and they can go over the map
with him. The Benders approach--what are they up to? The
father confronts Flash, accusing him of stealing a box of
ten-gauge shotgun shells from their storeroom. Flash is
incensed at being accused of thievery, but Speed tries to get
to the bottom of it. Bender says he had a box of shells in
his storeroom, and saw Flash cleaning a shotgun and
loading it. Speed informs Bender they don't even have a
ten-gauge shotgun with them, and besides, Flash wouldn't
steal. Rip Bender, who has apparently wandered off,
returns and tells his father he must have been mistaken.
Rip says, "Sure--the old man must have lost his head. He
knows better than that." Both Benders then apologize for
accusing Flash, and Speed and Jimmy prepare to leave.
Rip asks, "Where you boys headed for this morning?"
Speed replies, "Oh, we're taking a swing over west of here.
If we find a likely spot, we may set down and do some
hunting." We hear the plane's engine starting, and they take
off. Rip and his father discuss how beautifully their plan
worked--Rip has planted a bomb on the plane while Jimmy,
Speed and Flash were distracted by the old man's
accusations! The sound effects of a plane are heard under
the conversation between Jimmy and Speed, who are
looking at the ground for signs of Ortez. Jimmy makes a
short bank to get a better look at the ground and sees
something hanging down from the landing gear. It looks
like a box. Speed crawls out on the wing for a better look.
"Fly in a straight line at about half throttle." Speed manages

to get out on the wing, and gets ahold of the mysterious box. "Great guns, Jimmy, it's a time bomb! It's set to explode at 8:30!" Jimmy cries out, "Oh gosh, Speed, it's about 8:30 now!" Speed asks for a knife to cut the rope, but Jimmy doesn't have one--they'll have to bail out! But Jimmy discovers a hand-axe (standard flying equipment?) in the cockpit, and Speed tries to cut the rope. "Can you make it, Speed?" "I don't know, Jim! Look out!" Then the sound effect of an explosion, and this is where the listeners are left, in true cliffhanger fashion, not knowing whether or not their heroes have cut the rope in time. The announcer returns to close: "So---this is the cunning and deadly scheme conceived by Rip Bender. What will happen to Jimmy and Speed? Don't miss the next episode of *The Air Adventures of Jimmy Allen!"* Another promo for the program aimed at potential sponsors follows, and the show closes with the music theme.

A good script makes or breaks the show, and this is one of the better ones from the earlier programs of the Children's Hour. There is plenty of action, lots of sound effects, and fairly good dialogue. The voices of the actors "sound" like the characters, except for Speed, who sounds much too mature to be a boy. The voice of Flash Lewis leaves the impression the character is slow-witted; whether this is intended isn't known. Certainly the ending is designed to keep the kids tuning in. They could also join "Jimmy Allen Flying Clubs." The show was syndicated; perhaps if it had been on a network and had a steady sponsor, its run would have been longer.

THE AMERICAN SCHOOL OF THE AIR (SCHOOL OF THE AIR OF THE AMERICAS)

This was truly the first real attempt at broadcasting

an educational program for children, and it pre-dated the earliest "thrillers" by a year. The show began in February of 1930 sponsored by the Grisby-Grunow Company for the purpose of selling radios (similar to what RCA was doing), but CBS kept it as a sustaining program when the sponsorship was dropped (Atkinson, 1942). In fact, CBS kept the show on the air until 1948, making it one of the longer-running children's programs. The network put quite a bit of effort into *The American School*--teaching manuals were prepared in conjunction with the programs, and some of the network's top writing and acting talent worked on the programs. Included on the show were music appreciation, history, geography, literature, science and current events. In 1940, CBS expanded it to include Latin-American countries (over the new CBS Pan-American Network), and it became known as *The School of the Air of the Americas*. The show was now translated into Spanish. The programs were 30 minutes long, and were scheduled during the school day until 1945 when it was moved to late afternoon. Educator Josette Frank wrote in 1949 that the show was finally dropped due to the fact that all schools were still not equipped with radio sets (Frank, 1949). However, in retrospect and in view of the program's successful 18-year run, it appears more likely that CBS was channeling its efforts towards television.

The program of November 24, 1936, began with a trumpet call, followed by this announcement (with a British accent): *"The American School of the Air* takes pleasure in presenting the most celebrated love story of all literature--the tragedy of *Romeo and Juliet,* by William Shakespeare. (String music comes in and fades under) In this special radio adaptation of *Romeo and Juliet* by William Shakespeare, the *American School of the Air* presents two of the most famous lovers and some of the most beautiful lines in the scroll of English literature. The scene is laid in the ancient city of Verona, where two of its noblest houses, the Montagues and the Capulets, have for generations been nursing a family feud." The announcer goes on to set the scene for the famous story, when a fight in the streets of Verona between the two families is broken up by the Prince of Verona. Then we go to the masquerade ball, where Romeo has gone to be with Juliet. We hear the chamber music in the background over the two lovers' conversation. The narrator returns to set the next scene, where Romeo has climbed the wall to stand under Juliet's balcony, and we hear the familiar words of this scene. The narrator once again returns to set the scene for the third act when Juliet's vengeful cousin seeks Romeo. After this scene, in which Juliet's cousin is killed, Romeo is banished, and Juliet is reviled by her parents for refusing to marry Paris. She goes to Friar Lawrence for counsel, and he gives her the potion which will make everyone think she is dead. She takes the potion, but the Friar's messenger doesn't get the word to Romeo and we hear the tomb scene. The music comes up, and the narrator concludes with, *"The American School of the Air* has just presented an adaptation of William Shakespeare's immortal story, *Romeo and Juliet.* The next adaptation of Shakespeare will be *The Taming of the Shrew.* Tomorrow, the *American School of the Air* presents their geography broadcast on Denmark. Further information about programs will be found in the teacher's manual and classroom guide, copies of which may be procured, free of charge, by writing to *The American School of the Air,* 485 Madison Avenue, New York, New York." The music comes up to close.

The actors performing "Romeo" and "Juliet" were unnamed, but appeared to be experienced Shakepearian players. The production was extremely well done, and must have been highly appreciated by the teachers in the schools where it was used.

BOBBY BENSON AND THE
B-BAR-B RIDERS

Bobby Benson was originally a contemporary of Little Orphan Annie, and was also a juvenile character. Bobby was the pre-adolescent owner of a ranch in the Texas Big Bend area. With his loyal ranch hands (all the Children's Hour ranch hands were loyal to the death), Bobby set out as early as 1932 to solve mysteries. The early show was actually called *Bobby Benson's Adventures,* and was heard on CBS through 1936. The young cowboy hero came back to the air on Mutual in 1949 as *Bobby Benson and the B-Bar-B Riders.* The early version was a 15-minute serial, complete with the necessary cliffhanger endings; whereas the later version featured 30-minute scripts, with the stories complete in each episode.

Bobby may have been popular with the kids; probably less so with their parents. The early magazine articles protesting the children's thriller dramas usually named *Bobby Benson* as one that was objectionable, not only because of the crime theme, but the contests and prizes. A *Scribner's Magazine* article describes one of them: "The bait of this program is a yellow bandana of calico sent through the mail for membership. The yellow comes out on the child's neck. One corner of the kerchief dipped in a glass of water turned the liquid a lemon color. To obtain the remaining 9 pieces of the cowboy outfit, the child must send 9 boxtops and $3.60, or 87 boxtops alone. At 20 portions to the box, it would take a child five years, eating oatmeal every day, to save 87 package tops!" (Mann,

1933, p. 314).

A *Newsweek* article reported on a meeting of the Child Study Association. The association charged that "these programs feature 'adenoid juvenile actors' who speak bad grammar and read 'gun-barking melodramas that scare children.'" The article went on to describe a Bobby Benson episode. "Giving weight to the charge was Bobby Benson's program, sponsored by H-O. This week announcers told how Bobby's Aunt Lilly came to the ranch from Boston in an airplane. The plane is stolen by the villain, Little Snake. At the scene of the crime are footprints of a club-footed man. Cowboy Harka is captured by Little Snake, but Bobby's rangers are in hair-raising, hot pursuit" ("Protest: Adults condemn," 1934, p. 27). But Stedman (1971), in *The Serials,* describes the early shows as lighthearted in their approach, and incorporating some educational elements such as facts about the Big Bend country.

The regulars on the old ranch, besides Bobby, were Tex Mason, the foreman, Windy Wales, the aforementioned Harka who was an Indian, Diogenes Dodwaddle, Polly (another child), a Chinese cook and Aunt Lilly. Bobby was played part of the time by Billy Halop *(The Dead End Kids),* several parts were played by Tex Ritter, Don Knotts played Windy, and Polly was played by Florence Halop (recently deceased, and featured on several television series, including *Night Court* and *St. Elsewhere)* (Terrace, 1981). Eisenberg's (1936) book also described some of the programs: "The villain is Little Snake, leader of a Mexican band of desperadoes, who connives to get hold of a gold mine discovered by Bart's Uncle. Things are always happening at the ranch. Each episode ends with a note of suspense. Considerable local color and many ranch songs are used in these broadcasts"

(p. 204). These early shows were sponsored by H-O Cereals, and so Bobby's ranch was called the H-Bar-O at that time. These written descriptions of the first version will have to suffice; the search for an early episode was unsuccessful.

However, one of the later shows, broadcast August 15, 1950, has some differences. H-O Cereals had dropped sponsorship, and the ranch became the B-Bar-B. The 30-minute show was a complete story, titled "The Wise Monkeys." It begins with the announcer: "Here they come! They're riding fast and they're riding hard! It's time for action and adventure in the modern West with *Bobby Benson and the B-Bar-B Riders!* (Sound effects: galloping horses) And out in front, astride his golden palomino Amigo, it's the cowboy kid himself, Bobby Benson!" The hoofbeats come up again and Bobby cries, "Beeee-Barrrr-Beeeeeee!" Other voices are heard yelling, the music comes in, and fades under the announcer, "Today's mysterious adventure, The Three Wise Monkeys! (Music: up and under) Today's adventure begins some miles from the B-Bar-B Ranch, in a small cottage on the outskirts of Texas City. It's just after nightfall, and the lone rider makes his way up the brick road toward the cottage." He sets the scene by describing how the horse and rider stay to the middle of the road to avoid the mysterious shadows from each side. The rider reaches the house, dismounts and goes in (talking to the horse all the time). The door is unlocked and it's dark inside. He sees someone. "Agatha, you home, dear? It's me, Hiram." But it's not Agatha, and the intruder hits the man and knocks him out. The scene shifts to the next morning at the ranch. Bobby and a ranch hand named Irish are leaning against a corral and talking. Tex comes up and tells them about the attack on Hiram, one of the Peters boys. Hiram is complaining about the inefficiency of the law, so the sheriff has asked Tex to help. Of course Bobby and Irish go along. After a music bridge, we hear Hiram say, "Oh, my head! My poor achin' head!" Irish tells Hiram he's lucky he wasn't murdered. Hiram moans and complains, but finally explains he thought his wife, who was visiting her mother, had come home early. He doesn't know of any reason for the attack, for nothing was stolen---nothing, that is, except his monkey! Not a live monkey, but a china monkey, the one with his paws over his eyes--"See no evil." Hiram explains that his Uncle Hardrock left it to him when he died, and the other two monkeys to his two cousins (he has no use for the cousins). Tex suspects that the monkeys hold some clue to the old man's fortune, which was never found. Whoever took the monkey will be after the other two! Tex says he will phone the other two cousins to tell them of the danger. Then they all ride to the home of Bull, one of the other cousins. On the way, Hiram keeps complaining about not being left any of his Uncle's fortune, and blaming it on cousins Bull and Luke. "It's their fault my uncle didn't leave us his money. He said he wouldn't leave us anything because none of 'em were any good. But actually, it's those other two, Luke and Bull, that are no good. There's certainly nothin' bad about me!" When they get to Bull's house, they find the door open, and Bull knocked out on the floor. Tex finds pieces of china on the floor, "Looks like they're all that's left of the second monkey."

It's time for a break, and we hear the announcer give a promo for Bobby's latest contest. "All you have to do is send in a name for Tex Mason's horse, along with a drawing, a cutout, a photograph, or a picture cut out of a magazine, and you may win one of hundreds of wonderful prizes." The prizes included Bobby Benson bicycles, western outfits, and other western clothes and toys. After the promo, the last scene is repeated; they revive Bull and he tells them that he had opened the door, because the caller had identified himself as Tex Mason. Bull is belligerent, and accuses first Tex, then Hiram of slugging him. After they calm him down, he says he was the one who broke open the monkey to see what was inside--just a piece of paper with "writin' on it." The paper is gone, so whoever slugged Bull must have gotten it. Bobby asks if Bull read it. "Yeah, I read it all right, but it didn't make no sense to me. It just had a big number three on it, and the words, 'One hundred paces north of location two, and dig under flat rock.' It didn't make no sense to me." Of course, Tex and the others figure out that this must be a treasure map of where old Uncle Hardrock buried his fortune. Of course the three cousins who disliked each other would have to co-operate to get the treasure (apparently an unlikely occurrence). Hiram believes it must have been Luke, so they ride for Luke's ranch to see what he has to say about it. On the way, they meet Harka and Waco, who had been sent to look after Luke. They tell the riders that no one was there, and the place was locked up when they arrived, so they came to find Tex and Bobby and the others. Now it does look as though Luke is the guilty one. But when they arrive at Luke's ranch, someone leaves the house and rides away. They try to catch him, but too late--he got away. They return to Luke's ranch, and Tex goes inside. "Bobby--Bobby, don't come in here--stay outside!" They don't want Bobby to see that the furniture has been smashed, and there's blood all over everything. Now it looks as though Luke is a victim! After the announcer promos Bobby's appearance at the fair in Chicago, we return to the exciting climax! Hiram is still thinking only of the fortune, and doesn't care that his cousin has apparently been brutally murdered. Tex thinks it odd that the first two victims weren't really hurt and that Luke has been violently murdered. Harka comes out of the house. "Maybe he fool white man, but not fool Indian!" This confirms Tex's suspicions, and they ride for the railway station. They arrive just in time to stop Luke from boarding the train. Luke had staged his own death by smearing animal blood all over the house (this is what Harka was talking about). Bull and Hiram have gone to search for the treasure, but when they return, they are crestfallen--all they found was a box with a piece of paper in it. Mason reads it: "This is to notify the finder of this box that I, Hardrock Peters, have arranged prior to my death, for all my fortune to be turned over to various worthy charities secretly. I am, however, leaving a clue to the location of this box for each of my worthless nephews in the hope that they'll kill each other off trying to get it, and thus save the state this eventual expense. In any event, I shall at least die happy, knowing I've had this one last joke at their expense." Tex tells Hiram and Bull that Uncle Hardrock left them something--a lesson to be learned from the three wise monkeys--"See no evil, speak no evil, hear no evil. There's a lesson in that, boys--a lesson in why you didn't get a fortune." The announcer concludes the show, after the music bridge. *"The B-Bar-B Riders* is produced by Herbert Rice and directed by Bob Novak. Script was by Jim Sheen, and music by Ernestine Holmes. This is Bucky Coslow speaking, and reminding you that you're riding the trails to adventure and excitement while you hear that familiar cry, 'Beeee-Barrrr-Beeeeee!' (Music comes up) This program came from New York."

There was certainly plenty of action and violence in this Bobby Benson episode, not to mention plenty of blood (even if it did turn out to be that of an animal--and how could an Indian tell the difference between human and animal blood, anyway?). At least the child, Bobby, was spared the gruesome sight of all this blood by the adults, no doubt adding fuel to the imaginations of the young listeners--if it was too awful for Bobby to look at, it must have really been bad! The script seems to have followed a format almost more suitable for a serialized program. After each of the two breaks for promos, the entire story synopsis was given, and the last scene was repeated. Otherwise, the scripting and dialogue was good, with one conversation devoted to the heat of the Big Bend country and how they must take it easy on the horses in this heat. The voices of the actors were distinctive enough to tell them apart. Tex has the straight, "good" voice; Irish a hint of brogue; Hiram has the "old prospector" voice; Bull the voice of the big, dumb oaf; Harka sounded like Tonto; and Bobby's voice was that of a ten-year-old. There were plenty of sound effects, mostly hoofbeats. There never seemed to be any explanation of how a child came to own a ranch, or who took care of him. The young listeners could identify with Bobby as a child, but would have to use their imaginations to put themselves in his place. *Bobby Benson* was on the air through 1955, making it one of the last two thrillers on the air. The other was *Sergeant Preston of the Yukon* (Stedman, 1971).

BUCK ROGERS IN THE 25TH CENTURY

Another of the very early thrillers for children, and the first to use the space theme, was the story of the modern-day Rip Van Winkle, Buck Rogers. He was a World War I veteran who slept for 500 years and awoke in the year 24-something. Buck, like some of the other early radio characters, came from the comics to the airwaves in 1932 over CBS in a 15-minute serial, and then to the movie

serials in 1939. Buck fought 25th century evil on land and
in space, and was joined in his fight by the brilliant Dr.
Huer, scientist and inventor, the beautiful lieutenant Wilma
Deering, and sometimes, the Martian Black Barney. The
evil Killer Kane was, more often than not, the villain of the
show. Some of the early reviewers of children's radio were
not pleased with Buck's adventures (too much
"skulduggery"), although some did concede that the
imaginary world of the future and Dr. Huer's fantastic
inventions were stimulating to youngsters' imaginations.
One reviewer, while conceding that Buck was a "Lindbergh
type," worried about Buck's lack of a visible means of
support (Mann, 1933). Perhaps it came from the many
premiums offered by the show, including badges, Buck
Rogers pocket watches, a disintegrator gun, and a
friction-powered rocket ship.

The show left the air in 1936, and returned in 1939,
still as a 15-minute serial. The show used the 30-minute
format later in its run. The returning episode, of April 4,
1939, fulfilled the obligation of letting new listeners
unfamiliar with Buck's appearance in the 25th century
know just how he came to be there--without repeating the
first episode. *"Buck Rogers--in the 25th Cennn---tury!*
(Sound effects: rocket ship blasting off) Buck Rogers is
back on the air! Buck and Wilma and all their fascinating
friends and mysterious enemies in the super scientific 25th
century. This program is brought to you by the makers of
those delicious confections on a stick, Popsicle, Fudgsicle
and Creamsicle. Now I have a swell surprise for you--the
famous winner of the typical American Boy contest has
now become Popsicle Pete!" Then we receive a message
from Popsicle Pete (a young actor who stumbled several
times over the word "Popsicle"). "And now for Buck
Rogers and his thrilling adventures, 500 years in the future.

As you probably know, Buck was born here in our own time, in this 20th century. The story of how he got started in his amazing adventures so far in the future is mighty interesting. But instead of telling you about it, let's turn the dial that will project us ahead in time and find out all about it that way. Now the capital of 25th century America is Niagra. And there it is that Dr. Huer, the great scientist, has his marvelous laboratory. In one room of it, he's working on a strange-looking device that sends a peculiar greenish light down onto a human figure lying on a table before him. Shall we join him there? Okay then, here we go--500 years into the future!" Wilma enters, sees the figure lying there and is obviously worried. But Dr. Huer reassures her that Buck is merely asleep; "under the influence of electro-hypnotic rays." Wilma asks, "What's that thing near his head that looks like a miniature power-plant with a loudspeaker on top if it?" Dr. Huer explains that this is the "electro-hypnotic mem-telephone," a device which will (conveniently) allow memory to come verbally through the loudspeaker, a device that had its beginnings in the 20th century. Wilma obviously has a low opinion of her ancestors. "I always thought the people back in the 20th century weren't much better than savages." (Excepting Buck, presumably.) She is reassured by Dr. Huer, who names off the great scientists of the early part of the 20th century. Wilma is unconvinced. "They never really got anywhere with rocket ship development or anything like that." (The writer, Jack Johnstone, may have had a great imagination, but not much faith in his contemporaries.) Dr. Huer goes on with the experiment, trying to explain how it works to Wilma, who doesn't understand. Dr. Huer asks the sleeping figure, "Young man, what is your name?" A voice replies, "Buck Rogers." Wilma is astounded, for the voice came from the loudspeaker and Buck's lips didn't move! Dr. Huer asks how Buck happened to come to the 25th century, and the story is repeated: how Buck, in the year 1919, was in the lower workings of an abandoned mine near Pittsburgh. The mine caved in, releasing a peculiar gas which put him in a state of suspended animation. Then the ground shifted, letting in fresh air, and he woke up in the 25th century. Dr. Huer asks how Buck knew it was the 25th century. Buck replies, "I was told what year it was by Lt. Wilma Deering, a beautiful girl soldier I met--the finest and bravest girl I've ever met." Wilma is embarrassed by this line of questioning, and changes the subject. Buck continues, "Thanks to Dr. Huer, the greatest scientist that ever lived; the man who invented the first rocket ship that took us to the moon." Now it is Dr. Huer's turn to be embarrassed, and he tells Buck to wake up. Buck apologizes for falling asleep, but is assured that the test went well and that he didn't say anything he shouldn't have. They discuss Buck's love of excitement, and Dr. Huer's newest invention, a rocket ship device that allows limitless speed for rocket ships; then they hear something coming their way. A loud crash ends the day's episode, and the announcer's voice is heard. "Say--Buck's wish for excitement certainly came true in a hurry. Great day! I wonder what that was. I certainly hope he and Wilma and Dr. Huer are all right! What do you say, Popsicle Pete?" Pete and the announcer talk about saving Popsicle bags for wonderful free prizes like cameras, dolls, sweatshirts, gorgeous jewelry, and the like. The show ends with the rocket ship sound effects.

In the world of children's radio, there was little overt romance, and most of the programs bent over backwards to make sure everything was on the up and up. However, the relationship between Buck and Wilma was suspect, with a seeming undercurrent of feelings under the stilted dialogue. After all, they did spend a lot of time together, on land and in the spaceships! *Buck Rogers in the 25th Century* lasted off and on until 1947, making it one of the longer-running children's adventures. The show was also on television in 1950.

CAPTAIN MIDNIGHT

Perhaps the best known of the Children's Hour aviators was Captain Albright, a World War I hero who had become known as "Captain Midnight," and spent his life fighting crime in all parts of the world. The show was first heard on WGN in 1939, then on Mutual beginning on September 30, 1940. *Captain Midnight* was one of the few programs that stuck with the 15-minute serialized format into the late 1940's (Dunning, 1976).

The first episode explained the nickname, and how Captain Midnight became the leader of the Secret Squadron. The program's open began with sound effects of a bell tolling, "Bong--bong--bong--bong" and then the sound of a plane comes closer. Then over the sound effects, the slow, ponderous tones of announcer Pierre André, *"Captain-----Midnight!* Brought to you by the makers of Ovaltine!" Then more bell gongs (totaling 12) as the sound of the plane fades away. Then André picks up the pace somewhat, *"Captain Midnight,* brought to you every day by the makers of Ovaltine." After extolling the virtures of Ovaltine, "your favorite food drink," he advises the youngsters to "tell mother you'd like to have Ovaltine every day, and listen to this swell new program." The narration sets the scene--it's in France, during World War I. In a candle-lit room, two men discuss the mission ("to save France") the young captain is to attempt. "The odds against him are about 100 to one." As he knocks on the door, the commander blows out the candle so that he will not know the identity of the aviator he is sending to begin a long and dangerous task that hopefully will lead to the extermination of Ivan Shark, "the most rascally and dangerous criminal in the world." The young captain says, "If I do not return by 12 o'clock, you will know I have failed." We hear the plane take off. Time passes, and the two men inform us it is now 15 seconds to midnight. Of course this is the cue for the sound of the approaching plane; and, from now on, "he shall be known as Captain Midnight." The adventure resumes 20 years later, during which time a shadowy plane and a mysterious pilot would appear, "whenever trouble started in any part of the world, certain to come diving furiously from the night sky." The narration sets the scene, on an estate in Virginia, where a car drives up to a large stone house. Captain Midnight gets out, goes to the door, the door is answered and a conversation ensues which consists of an elaborate code. Captain Midnight is then given instructions on where he is to go in the house, leading him through secret passageways, and down a circular staircase, where he awaits instructions. Another car drives up, carrying three men. One goes into the house, where he speaks with "SS-11," who tells him Captain Midnight is waiting. After putting on the mask he carries in his pocket, he meets with the Captain, and we find out that the mysterious aviator's real name is Captain Albright, and that he has been on vacation in the Orient with his ward, Chuck Ramsey; during his absence a secret anti-American criminal organization has come into being. The Secret Squadron is being formed, and Captain Midnight will be the leader. The unnamed leader takes off his mask, and writes his name on a piece of paper, causing Captain Midnight to gasp at the revelation. Pierre André returns to ask the listeners, "If you like the program, keep on spreading the news to all the fellows and girls you know." And, of course, drink Ovaltine. "Be sure to tune in tomorrow, same time, same station for another stirring adventure of *Captain Midnight,* brought to you every day, Monday through Friday, by the makers of Ovaltine. (The bell and plane sound effects sneak in under the close.) This is Pierre André, your announcer, telling you goodbye---and happy---landing!" (Bell and plane sound effects come up to close.)

In spite of the fact that a little simple arithmetic would show Captain Midnight to be a man in his 40's, young boys found a hero they could identify with. After all, this was an ordinary human, with no super powers. And perhaps even better, another sidekick was added, Secret Squadron member (SS-3) Joyce Ryan. Ah, at last a heroine who shared in the adventures and gave the girls in the audience someone they could identify with. The young ward, Chuck Ramsey, was SS-2, and the other regular character was the mechanic Ichabod "Icky" Mudd. Kids could join, or form, Secret Squadrons, and among the program premiums was a secret decoder badge, which enabled the listeners to decipher the messages at the end of the day's episode. Groups of Secret Squadron members would gather to listen during the week, and write down the code message, which was then translated with the aid of the decoder badge. Now you were one of the elite--a Secret Squadron member who *understood* what was going on!

A later episode, broadcast June 9, 1941, started much the same way as the series premiere, with the bell tolling and the sound of the plane coming closer. "The makers of Ovaltine present--*Captaaaaain Midnight!* (sound effects come up) *Captain Midnight,* brought to you every day, Monday through Friday, at this same time, by the makers of Ovaltine. But first, another important announcement from Captain Midnight himself. So stand by for a personal message from Captain Midnight. Here he is." We hear Captain Midnight telling the young listeners to buy Defense Savings Stamps, or to write in for more information about Uncle Sam's Defense Savings Stamps and Defense Savings Bonds. "And now, for our adventure. Last time, all available Secret Squadron planes flew to Sector 86 in the Caribbean Sea, where Pilot SS-39 had sighted a submarine and dropped his bomb. In the submarine were Ivan Shark and one of his lieutenants, Barnoff. Seriously damaged by Agent SS-39's bombs, the other sea boat remained submerged till after dark, and then rose to the surface and radioed a desperate call for help to Ivan Shark's Caribbean island base. A second submarine was dispatched to the rescue, and the two boats made contact shortly before daybreak, but only after flashing signal lights. Now, as our present scene opens, one submarine is lying stationary, rocked gently by the small waves. A second submarine is approaching the first, its conning tower dimly visible. At the wheel of the first submarine stands its commander, Captain Mueller. And close to him is the master spy, Ivan Shark, talking in low tones." They plan to transfer everyone to the rescue sub, and set a time bomb on the damaged one, to make Captain Midnight think that they are dead. We join Captain Midnight and his mechanic, Ichabod Mudd, flying over and searching for the sub. They see two small boats, and call Chuck (SS-2), but then one boat disappears. Captain Midnight thinks something is fishy--he can't see anyone on deck, and why is the sub just lying on the surface? He calls all squadron members to investigate the sub. Suddenly the sub explodes! Captain Midnight realizes the sub was scuttled and the crew has escaped. He calls all squadron members to search the ocean. They return to base, where Chuck is puzzled about what happened to the crew--Chuck proposes that there may have been two submarines, and Captain Midnight realizes he is right! The narrator concludes by telling us that Ivan Shark and his accomplices are distributing the bombs that will destroy the hemisphere defenses if Captain Midnight doesn't stop them. "Well, we may find out more about that in a minute from the secret clue we have for you tonight." After an Ovaltine commercial, "And now, here's that clue for tomorrow's adventure in Master Code Number Six. Are you ready? Here's the first word--14, 11, 8, 25, 23, 3, 14. Okay, did you get that? Here's the second word--16, 9, 2, 26, 14, 3, 9. Just one more word, the third and last--here it is. 22, 2, 25, 10, 12, 1. Now remember, set your Mystery Dial Codeograph for Master Code Number Six, and figure out the secret message about tomorrow's adventure. And tune in tomorrow, same time, same station, for *Captain Midnight!* (Sound effects: plane and bell) Until then, this is Pierre André, your Ovaltine announcer, saying goodbye and happppy laaaaaannnnding!"

A third episode, from June 16, 1941, was part of the same story line. Captain Midnight and the Secret Squadron have attacked Ivan Shark's island hideout with dive bombers. Icky Mudd and Chuck Ramsey have landed a photographic amphibian near the island and they take off so that they can take pictures of the damage. But Ivan Shark is safe in his control center, which is carved out of solid rock--there are planes on a lower level, which have not been damaged, and the underground harbor has not been damaged. Shark tells his henchman of plans to attack Captain Midnight's secret base on Puerto Rico. Meanwhile, Captain Midnight, Joyce and Chuck are looking at the picture, searching for an underground hangar. He is planning to drop 50 parachute troops accompanied by landing barges to attack Shark. Icky tells him they need a pilot for the 8 o'clock patrol over Shark's island--Captain Midnight sends Chuck, and consents to let Joyce go along as an observer, because nothing has happened to any of the patrols. But the announcer comes in to tell us that tonight will be different--Ivan Shark will send ten fighter planes to attack the patrol. After an Ovaltine commercial, the code is given for Flight Commanders only, in their own special code, which is inside the Flight Commander's ring.

Captain Midnight was a hero whose time had come; world unrest and talk of war created the perfect background for the stories. With the entry of the United States into World War II, Captain Midnight and his Secret Squadron fought the Axis, who had been joined by the notorious Ivan Shark. (The really bad guys always became traitors.) The young Secret Squadron members could at least imagine they were doing their part to fight the war. There was always plenty of excitement and action in the episodes, and sound effects of planes, bombs, and guns--plus cliffhanger endings that almost always left one member or another of the Secret Squadron in real danger. The show began to diminish in popularity after the war was over, and lasted through 1949. Captain Midnight made it to the big screen in a 1942 movie serial, and was later on television as a 30-minute show from 1954 until 1958.

CHANDU, THE MAGICIAN

This adventure serial was usually set in exotic locales where Frank Chandler (better known as Chandu) could use the supernatural powers he had learned from a yogi in India. Frank, his sister Dorothy Regent, and her children Bob and Betty traveled far and wide in search of adventure. According to Dunning (1976), the first episodes were devoted to a search for Dorothy's husband, who had been lost in a shipwreck. The show began in 1932 on the West Coast on the Don Lee Network, then went to Mutual for its first run, through 1936. The early shows were 15-minute serialized stories, apparently designed for a mixed audience. Eisenberg's (1936) brief program description gave the time of broadcast over WOR in New York as 8:00-8:15 PM; nonetheless the show was popular with the youngsters in the audience. *Chandu* is one of the shows usually mentioned in the early articles protesting program content (not surprising in view of the plot emphasis on the occult). It is also mentioned in those surveys listing the popularity of radio programs with children in the 1930's.

The magician was another radio character who was also on the silver screen--first in a 1932 Fox feature; then in a 1934 serial which was later adapted to a book. The famous screen villain, Bela Lugosi, played the "bad guy" in the *Chandu* feature film; then graduated to the role of Chandu himself in the serials. This was one of the few "good guy" roles ever attempted by Lugosi.

Chandu returned to Mutual for another run in 1948, becoming a 30-minute show, and winding up in 1950 on ABC. Some of the other characters appearing in the shows were Roxor the villain, and the Egyptian Princess Nadji, Chandu's love interest.

The tape of an early episode broadcast in 1935 is lacking in two things--there really is no open and close, and Chandu (Frank Chandler) is absent from the script, with the action carried by Dorothy, Bob and Betty. Terrace (1981) in *Radio's Golden Years,* gives this description of a typical Chandu opening:

Sound Effect: A large gong sounding. Announcer: (over music) *Chandu, the Magician.* Good evening, ladies and gentlemen. The makers of White King Granulated Soap present for your enjoyment tonight and every weekday evening at this time *Chandu, the Magician.* Listen and you will travel to strange lands, you will thrill to high adventure, romance, and mystery...There are many tales told on radio, but only one Chandu; there are many soaps on your grocer's counter, but none like White King...Now let the play begin..." (p. 52).

The 1935 episode then continues with the theme music (with a definite Oriental flavor), and the gong. The announcer sets the scene: "In his study in the house in Sartabaya, Frank Chandler receives a call from Jeffrey Marshall, the young Englishman who was a guest at the Palace of the Secret Star. Marshall tells Chandler a witch doctor in Africa pronounced an incantation, which compelled him to come to Java, to the palace of Beatrice, and he has been unable to leave. Chandler promises to help him. But as they talk, a weird hypnotic sound is heard and, as if in a trance, Jeffrey rises and walks from the room. The present act opens in the observatory of Beatrice Palace, several days later. *Channnnn-du--the Magician!"* The gong is heard again, then the voices of Betty, Bob and Dorothy. They are discussing the strange maps on the wall of the observatory, and wishing Beatrice would get there soon. Betty wishes Uncle Frank had come too, but Dorothy tells her that Beatrice just invited them. Beatrice enters--he is a somewhat sinister-sounding character. Bob asks him about a particular map on the wall, and is told, "That, my dear young man, is Lemuria." Lemuria is an island that supposedly disappeared centuries ago (similar to Atlantis) and Bob says he never heard of it until they were on the island of Lura. Dorothy interrupts, and it is obvious she doesn't want them discussing what happened on Lura in front of Beatrice. He offers to show them some pictures of Lemuria while they are waiting for it to get dark enough to look through the telescope. This is a book of drawings, which he *knows* came from Lemuria. He gets the book down and puts it on a table. Bob says, "Look--on the cover--that funny drawing." Almost to herself, Dorothy says, "The seal of Solomon." Beatrice replies, "I am not surprised that you should know it, madam, but your son--" Bob explains that it was in the cave on the island, right over the door. The first drawing is of a "funny-looking building." Beatrice says it was the palace of the Lemurian king. "Sometimes, Mrs. Regent, those who are sensitive to such things, as they watch the pages of this book, may see one or another come to life, as if he who watched were walking in the streets of these forgotten cities or kneeling at the altars of forgotten gods." A strange sound is heard, and Beatrice says, "Look--at the pictures." Suddenly the three are in the palace, and Beatrice says, "Do not turn your eyes away. You will see that concerning which wise men have speculated about for countless thousands of years." Betty is scared, but Bob thinks it's keen. They enter the throne room, with trumpet sounds. Then everything begins to shake. "It's an earthquake." Sounds of screaming and the earthquake are heard, and then they are back to reality, looking at the picture which is just as it was before. Dorothy has apparently fainted, and Beatrice suggests they put her on the couch--"No doubt she will be herself in a moment or two." The gong is heard, followed by the theme music, but no closing. A typical closing is recounted in Terrace's book:

> "We pause before we say good evening to suggest that you and your family listen to *Chandu* every weekday evening at this time. Travel with us to strange places and faraway lands, into the mystery and intrigue of Egypt and the Near East. And of course we like to have you use the soap we make, White King granulated Soap...So, on your radio remember *Chandu, the Magician*...and at your grocer's remember White King Granulated Soap. Goodnight" (pp. 52-53).

The episode certainly met the cliffhanger criterion for the serials, although, like so many of the very early programs, there was not much action. The script was quite dependent on dialogue to carry the story line, with the sound effects suggesting the earthquake and the end of the island Lemuria. A tape for the later run was not located.

THE CINNAMON BEAR

Paddy O'Cinnamon, *The Cinnamon Bear,* and two children, Judy and Jimmy Barton, were the central characters of this Christmas story, told in 26 15-minute chapters. The show was syndicated and was first heard in 1937; then repeated yearly for an unknown number of years over many stations. The story line involves twins Judy and Jimmy's search for the missing Silver Star (a Christmas tree ornament) which Paddy tells them has been stolen by the Crazy Quilt Dragon. To recover it, they must go to Maybe Land, a fantasy place inhabited by dragons, pirates, giants, witches and various talking animals.

The story begins with the theme music, then "And

here's *The Cinnamon Bear!"* The announcer says, "And WSOY invites young and old alike to enjoy the adventures of Paddy O'Cinnamon, the Cinnamon Bear. By listener request, WSOY brings back this popular Christmas serial, Monday through Saturday evenings at 6:05. Join Judy and Jimmy and the Cinnamon Bear as they wander through Maybe Land, looking for the children's Silver Star to top the Christmas tree. Meet all the unusual people of Maybe Land, including Crazy Quilt Dragon, the Wintergreen Witch, FeFo the Giant, and the beautiful Melissa. Adventure, excitement, thrills and fun are in store for everyone who joins the Cinnamon Bear. Maybe Land is as large as your imagination, and it's waiting for you on these stations six nights a week until Christmas. We apologize in advance if the transcription is not what it should be--these records are 15 years old, and they're being presented now because many of you asked for it. Join us now for the adventures of *The Cinnamon Bear."* The theme music comes up, then, "This is the story of the Cinnamon Bear and his very marvelous adventures with Judy and Jimmy Barton. But we can't very well meet the Cinnamon Bear before we meet Judy and Jimmy. They are twins, and they live in a big, old-fashioned house. At this very minute, they are in the upstairs sitting room, and from all I can hear, Judy and Jimmy are busily engaged in that very pleasant task of writing letters to Santa Claus. Let's listen." Judy and Jimmy's mother enters, bringing the boxes of Christmas tree ornaments. But the Silver Star which tops the tree is missing! Perhaps it was put into the attic by mistake, and the children beg her to let them go up to look for it. In the trunk in the attic they find a crazy quilt and an old, tiny teddy bear with a green ribbon around his neck. When they look at the bear through an old telescope, the bear comes to life and sings a song, "I'm the Cinnamon

Bear." He tells them that the Crazy Quilt Dragon has taken the Silver Star, and offers to help them chase down the dragon, who has headed for the Lollipop Mountains. He tells them they must "de-grow" so that they will be four inches tall like him. He will show them how to do it. The theme music returns, followed by the announcer: "Let's be sure to listen next time, for Judy, Jimmy and the Cinnamon Bear." The theme music comes up to close.

The story is charming, a real opportunity for the young listeners to use their imaginations and follow Paddy O'Cinnamon (a bear with an Irish brogue) through Maybe Land. The show enjoyed a long run, probably well into the 1950's. (The tape was from 1952.) The scripting and acting were particularly good for 1930's vintage radio. *The Cinnamon Bear* was children's radio at its best.

THE CISCO KID

The western series adapted from O. Henry's stories about the Robin Hood of the West began on Mutual in 1942 with a 30-minute complete-in-one-episode format. Previously, a 1929 movie, *In Old Arizona,* had been made with the Kid as the hero. The show featured one of the few non-WASP characters to be the hero of a radio western. Cisco was always accompanied by his hefty sidekick, Pancho. Many of the other western heroes had sidekicks who were something other than white with Anglo-Saxon surnames, but the Cisco Kid stands alone as the central character who was a Mexican. Cisco's accent was slight, so he didn't sound *too* Mexican, but Pancho was allowed to have a heavier accent, being the sidekick and a somewhat comic character besides. Nonetheless, the show did encourage a more positive attitude toward minorities, just as Superman and some of the other Children's Hour

programs began to do in the 1940's. One episode of the
show, mentioned specifically by MacDonald (1979) in
Don't Touch That Dial!, even defended Indians (pp.
205-206).

The earlier shows departed from the traditional
children's format in that Cisco's reward for righting wrongs
was usually a kiss from the beautiful senorita. The other
westerns of the Children's Hour would never stoop to
include any of that mushy stuff! However, MacDonald also
said that the later version beginning in 1946 (which was
more successful) had eliminated much of this romance,
with ". . . Cisco toning down his functions as a Casanova
and paying stricter attention to chasing desperadoes" (p.
202).

The Cisco Kid episode to be described was dated
"somewhere between 1943 and 1945." However, because
the program lacks the opening described by Dunning
(1976) for the earlier shows, as well as no kisses from
beautiful senoritas, it was probably from 1946 or later (p.
134). The show began with the music theme, then the
announcer: "Here's adventure! Here's romance! Here's the
famous Robin Hood of the Old West!" (Sound effects:
galloping hoofbeats and rifle shots) Pancho cries,
"Ceesco---the shereeff! He ees getting closer!" Then Cisco,
"This way, Pancho! Vamanos!" The announcer intones,
"The Cisco Kid!" which is punctuated by a shot, then the
theme music comes back up. "Now, *The Cisco Kid,* and
our exciting story, 'Waters of the Flood.' It has long been
axiomatic that a moment of vanity has led to the undoing of
many a criminal. So it was when Park Sanders, gunman
and killer of the Old West, swore to show the Cisco Kid
who was the better man. As our story opens, Sanders and
his henchman, Jinks Doolin, are riding up to a store in the
town of Laurel." They enter the store, shoot and kill the old

storekeeper who is asleep behind the counter, and steal a box of ammunition. The shooting has been witnessed by a man across the street--the killers identify him as George Willard, who lives out along the river. "Come on, Jinks, we'll get him too!" George rides hard for home, with the killers in pursuit. He runs in the house and tells his wife Donna to get down the rifle. There is a gun battle, and Donna offers to get the other rifle and help--but the gunfire stops, and the killers go into George's shed after dynamite. They head up river to blow up the dam, which will wash George and Donna's home away--and them, too! Meanwhile, Cisco and Pancho have heard the gunfire, and see the killers riding up the river. They ride to the Willard's home to find out what has happened. George is urging Donna to get some things together so they can get away, but she refuses to leave her home. They hear Cisco and Pancho ride up, and Donna fires her rifle out the window at them. George cries, "Give me that rifle, Donna--that's the Cisco Kid and Pancho!" Donna apologizes for shooting at them. "Those fast shootin' pack rats was after George, so my trigger finger was kinda touchy, Cisco." They tell Cisco and Pancho about the dynamite, and the pair ride for the dam, but they're too late! Sanders and Doolin blow up the dam! They ride back to the ranch to get there before Sanders and Doolin, shooting as they ride. The killers grab George and ride off with him. Cisco is forced to give up his attack on the killers to rescue Donna, who has fallen in the path of the floodwaters and sprained her ankle. Here the show pauses, where apparently a commercial was to be inserted. Is Cisco too late? Of course he isn't, and Donna is rescued--they take her to Parson's ranch about a mile down the road. Meanwhile, the killers have George and plan to ambush Cisco--Sanders wants to capture him, and make Cisco and

Pancho watch while they murder Willard. Back at the Parson's ranch, the sheriff and his posse have come to see about the flood--Donna tells them that Cisco and Pancho are after the killers. The sheriff isn't too pleased about this turn of events, and they ride to meet Cisco. The sheriff tells them to get out of the county, but Cisco and Pancho refuse, and ride to find George and the killers. They circle the trail, and come up behind the killers. The killers see the sheriff and his posse coming up the trail and they decide to finish off Willard and kill the sheriff. But Cisco and Pancho arrive just in time to save Willard and capture Sanders and Doolin. The sheriff rides up and is about to arrest Cisco and Pancho, but Willard intervenes. "You don't know it, but Cisco here saved your life as well as mine. These two hombres was gonna dry-gulch you after they pushed me offa that ledge--and they'd have got you, too." Pancho asks the sheriff, "How much you theenk your life worth, shereef? It worth thanks to Ceesco for saving you, no?" The sheriff sheepishly thanks Cisco, and takes the prisoners to jail. The show ends with a conversation between the Willards and Cisco and Pancho--Donna says Cisco should be the sheriff, and she invites them to their home when they get a new one built. After a music bridge, we hear the standard ending, with the pun by Pancho--he is talking about their friend, Porfirio, who is going to work for the circus, "And make the beeg clean-up." Cisco asks, "What is he going to do, amigo?" Pancho replies, "Porfirio going to wash the elephants." Cisco groans, "Ohhh, Pancho!" Pancho comes back, "Oooo, Ceesco." They break into laughter, then, "Up, Diablo! Up, Loco!" More laughter, hoofbeats, and the theme music. The announcer concludes, "And so ends another exciting adventure with O. Henry's famous Robin Hood of the West, *The Cisco Kid!*" (Theme music up to end)

An action-packed script, indeed, with plenty of shooting and hard riding, and some really despicable criminals! The dialogue is fairly believable--but the plot asks us to believe that Cisco and Pancho could ride down the trail from the dam faster than the rushing floodwaters; a real feat! And Donna's refusal to leave her home with the flood almost a certainty seems out of character for one of the few self-sufficient women of the Old West that we have met in the Children's Hour. This is a real step forward in the elimination of bigotry in the children's programs--a courageous woman who isn't afraid and is willing to shoot to protect her man. The fact that Cisco has to rescue her because of an injury rather than fear doesn't really detract from the strength finally shown by a woman character. *The Cisco Kid* lasted until the early 1950's; documentation on the actual dates of broadcast is lacking. It was also a syndicated 30-minute television show in 1951.

DICK TRACY

Another comic strip character making a successful jump from the newspaper pages to the radio, then to four highly successful movie serials, and finally (not so successfully) to television in 1950 was the hawk-nosed detective, Dick Tracy. Based on Chester Gould's comic strip, *Tracy* went on the air as a 15-minute serial in 1935 on Mutual, then to NBC in 1937. It was off from 1939 to 1943, when another run, this time on NBC Blue (ABC), lasted until 1948. (A few 30-minute shows were run in 1946 on Saturday.) The series featured most of the comic strip characters, including Tracy's assistant, Pat Patton, his adopted son Junior, Flat Top, and Tess Trueheart. There were plenty of premiums to entice the kids, including a Dick Tracy watch and badges; not to mention membership in the Dick Tracy Secret Service Patrol. The amount of Quaker Oats kids could eat determined the rank they could achieve (Time-Life, 1969).

"And now---*Dick Tracy!*" (Sound effects: beep-beep-beep-beep-beep) "This is Tracy--on the Case of the Empty Safe. Stand by for action! Let's go, men!" (Sound effects: car and siren) "Yes, it's *Dick Tracy,* protector of law and order!" This particular episode of "The Case of the Empty Safe," was broadcast May 1, 1945, and following the introduction was a news bulletin informing us of the reports of Hitler's death. "And now, *Dick Tracy.* In yesterday's story, you saw how the evidence began to pile up, making Tracy sure that Spike Connally was responsible for the dynamiting of the empty safe. You remember, too, how Sergeant Martin, while distributing posters of the description of Spike and his girlfriend, reported to Tracy his suspicions concerning the occupants of a certain house. Jumping into the car, Dick and Pat were soon there. While Dick rang the front doorbell, Pat went around to the rear to forestall any escape from that direction. Inside, Spike and Gert didn't know of Pat's whereabouts, and they made their way slowly toward the rear of the house. Today, Spike and Gert are almost to the back door. Dick is still ringing the front doorbell. Listen." Pat nabs Spike and Gert, who play innocent. Pat tells them, "Stick out yer hands!" (Pat speaks with a hint of Irish brogue.) Gert whimpers, "Are ya gonna handcuff us?" Pat replies, "Well, these aren't exactly pearl bracelets." Spike jumps Pat, and they fight. Gert hits Pat over the head with her shoe, knocking him out. They run to the garage and escape by driving through the back wall as the sirens come closer. A car chase ensues (via sound effects) and they outrun the cops, only to run out of gas. A helpful motorist stops, is "knocked cold" by Spike and dragged into the bushes by Spike and Gert, who steal the hapless Good Samaritan's car. Then we hear Dick and Pat, who has recovered with only a bump on his head. (There was no such thing as a concussion on juvenile radio.) They are on the radio with headquarters, learning of the pair's escape. Tracy says, "Keep all men on 24-hour duty. Wait for instructions!" Dick and Pat head for the pair's destination, the farming district. "Strangers always attract attention in rural districts. We'll start questioning some of the natives--and I'll bet we'll soon run across a clue!" They stop to question a farmer, who seems reluctant to tell them anything. This, of course, along with a wink from the farmer, tells Tracy that Spike and Gert are in the farmhouse. The show breaks for a War Bond public service announcement, and returns to find Spike and Gert holding the farmer's own shotgun on him. Spike threatens, "If they come back, this guy gets it with this shotgun!" The announcer returns to close. "Quietly making their way back to their car, Dick and Pat began contacting all the patrol cars and giving them instructions. Be sure to tune in tomorrow, same time, same station, for the adventures of *Dick Tracy!* This is George Gunn speaking." A promo for the comic strip and the radio show followed.

An episode of "The Case of the Broken Window," aired September 13, 1946, found Tracy and Patton on the trail of two youthful jewel robbers, Spider and Mickey. After the standard opening, we find Dick and Pat in the rooming house formerly occupied by the two boys. Dick sees a nose-print on a window pane and has Pat remove the pane from the frame, for a yet-to-be-explained reason. Meanwhile, Spider and Mickey are looking for work, to get by until they can spot another job. They go to a factory which has been advertising for help, and the kindly owner hires them for $17.50 a week each, lifting boxes that weigh 40 pounds. Believing they are orphans, he gives them a

$2 advance so they can go to a boarding house. They work hard all week; Mickey is even entrusted with a bank deposit. At the end of the week, the owner gives them each $20 (a $2.50 raise). Mickey is pleased, but Spider says the guy would have had to pay twice as much to hire a man instead of two boys, and tells Mickey to pay attention to how much money is there the next time he's sent to the bank. The episode closes with: "Any top detective lives a life of danger, and double goes for Dick Tracy because he's the very top. Listen to another chapter of Dick Tracy's tangles with the underworld. Tune in at the same time, same station for the adventures of *Dick Tracy*."

Dick Tracy was probably one of the more violent kid's shows on the air; but there was never any doubt about who the bad guys were--they had names like "Spike" or "Spider" and they spoke with raspy voices and occasional lapses into bad grammar. They generally did no permanent bodily harm, certainly not to Tracy or Pat, but there was a lot of hitting people over the head to "knock them out." Of course, they never got away from the intrepid protector of law and order, and were always appropriately punished for their crimes. The young *Dick Tracy* listeners were urged to help the war effort in 1943, by pledging to fight waste.

> I pledge:
> 1. To save water, gas and electricity.
> 2. To save fuel oil and coal.
> 3. To save my clothes.
> 4. To save Mom's furniture.
> 5. To save my playthings
>   (MacDonald, 1975, p. 69).

DON WINSLOW OF THE NAVY

Another of the many comic strip heroes making his way to the air was the naval intelligence agent and aviator, Don Winslow. There were two runs of the show: the first, from 1937 through 1939, was a 15-minute five-day-a-week serial on NBC Blue. Dunning (1976) said the main theme of the first run was the pursuit of a worldwide crime organization headed by the Scorpion (p. 166). The second run (30-minute shows) began on October 5, 1942, and this time the enemy was real--the Japs and the Germans.

This episode (the first of the second run) began somewhat like *Captain Midnight*--with sound effects of a plane and a bell tolling. Then, "All hands on deck for *Don Winslow!* (Sound effects: machine-gun fire) Stand by for action--stand by for adventure--stand by for *Don Winslow of the Navy*--by the makers of delicious Post Toasties! Yes, shipmates, *Don Winslow* is on the air, bringing you the exciting adventures of the naval intelligence officers who fight against spies and saboteurs behind the lines so our great Navy can battle the enemy on the front lines. And now, shipmates, Commander Winslow's good friend and fellow officer is coming aboard. Here he is, Lieutenant Red Pennington." Pennington greets the listeners: "Hello, fellows and girls, it's sure great to be back! Boy, it seems like we've been away a long time. But now, we're all set for action again--and seriously, shipmates, this time it's worldwide action and it affects every one of us." He goes on to explain about the three fronts in the war, including the home front, where kids can help by staying healthy--naturally, by eating Post Toasties. "And now, shipmates, all hands on deck for our story. Don and Red are heading for a new assignment. As yet, they've not

received their fighting orders. They were just recalled from
shore leave and placed aboard a Navy PBY patrol bomber
bound for a secret rendezvous somewhere in the Pacific
Ocean. While on the way, their giant plane receives the
dreaded "SSS" signal from a large cargo liner, the
Redlands. That signal means "Submarine attack." They
turn back to go to the liner's aid--they spot the submarine
and roar down to the attack. (Sound effects: plane diving)
The bombardier sights--presses the trigger on the release
cable--and two bombs drop swiftly to the target!" (Sound
effects: explosions) Red is exulting the hit, but Don is
worried--it seems the sub is "too small." They spot a
survivor drifting away from the wreckage, and go down to
pick him up, as well as get a closer look at the remains of
the sub. The survivor was chief mate of the *Redlands,* and
is grateful for the rescue. They taxi over to get a look at the
wreckage, and Don finds what he's looking for--a piece of
the cabin liner that indicates the size of the sub. Don and
Red remember the intelligence information they got on
two-man subs, and they question the survivor. He tells
them that the cargo ship was carrying important cargo, and
was given secret orders that couldn't be opened until the
ship was an hour out of port. The ship was to stay out of
the regular shipping lanes. Don and Red realize that,
because of the short range of a two-man sub, the sinking
was deliberate. Don says, "The enemy is getting secret
information which is liable to destroy the whole convoy
command!" After a commercial for Post Toasties, the
announcer closes with, "Fellows and girls, be sure to be
with us every day to keep pace with the adventures of Don
and his friend, Red Pennington, as they track down the
dangerous enemies of our beloved country. Tomorrow,
Don and Red receive special secret orders from Admiral
Colby that will plunge them into one of the most thrilling

adventures of their entire careers. You'll hear all about it tomorrow--same time, same station, same call to action. (Sound effects: bosun's whistle) All hands on deck for *Don Winslow!* (echo) All hands on deck! *Don Winslow of the Navy* is presented Monday through Friday by the makers of nourishing Post Toasties, the delicious corn flakes that stay crisp longer in milk!"

Another episode, undated, but broadcast between 1942 and 1945, begins with Red Pennington talking about the naval bases and their importance to the fleet. After a Post Toasties commercial, the scene is set for the episode: (Sound effects of bosun's whistle) "All hands on deck! Yes, shipmates, all hands on deck for our story! Don and Red have received their orders from Admiral Waterman. Base H, one of the most important naval stations in the Pacific Ocean island defense range, is being threatened by a mysterious attack. Now--in our last episode, our friends learned that a new weapon had been developed by Dr. Franz Wolfe, and was being put to use by the enemy. It is the Blitzfan, a tiny flame only two feet long, controlled by radio, and able to carry a large and very deadly charge of explosives. The enemy is preparing to strike! We now join our friends as they are in a Navy Scout bomber, high over the Pacific, speeding to Base H." We join Don and Red discussing the merits of the Navy planes, and the two-man subs they're after. They figure that the subs, carrying the Blitzfans, must be based on a ship for re-fueling. Then we hear the voices of two of the enemy spies discussing the test of the Blitzfan. One is Von Korloff, spy chief, who speaks with a German accent. The other is Joseph, whom we presume was also German, but he speaks with a decidedly Mexican accent (he sounds like he belongs with *The Cisco Kid*). They discuss the plans--they will meet on the other side of the island with the Blitzfans. Herr Von

Korloff orders Joseph to get him a full report on the latest
Blitzfan that has been launched with a full load of
explosives. Von Korloff gloats: "Ah--this will be the
greatest success of my life! Those stupid fools, Winslow
and Pennington, thinking they could stop me! Heh, heh,
heh! The destruction of Base H will show them!" We return
to Don and Red, who are preparing to land at the base,
when Red sees something flashing in the sun. It's a
Blitzfan, headed straight for the island! They go in to blast
it with their machine guns! The device is hit, it blows up,
and then: "The elevators--and the rudder--don't answer!
They've been ripped to pieces! We're going down! Hang
on--we're too low to jump!" The announcer concludes the
day's episode: "Well, shipmates, Don and Red are certainly
in a tight spot! The concussion of the exploding Blitzfan
has wrecked their tail controls, and they're too low to use
their parachutes! How can they get down safely?" A Post
Toasties commercial follows, then: "Well, fellows and
girls, in their new adventure, Don and Red have already
come up against the work of the enemy. They have
succeeded in destroying a Blitzfan, but their plane is in
desperate trouble. So don't miss next Monday's thrilling
episode. Be on deck, same time, same station, same call to
action!"

     The two shows were full of sound effects, adding to
the realistic-sounding Navy jargon and information about
spies and secret weapons. There was certainly plenty of
action to keep the kids on the edge of their seats, and a
good cliffhanger ending to ensure that they'd be back for
the next episode. The actor's voices for Red and Don were
distinctive enough to be easily recognized, and sounded
right for the characters. The voice of the spy chief was
suitably villainous, with enough German accent to be
realistic, but the other spy's voice, with a Mexican accent,

was certainly out of place--perhaps they couldn't find another actor with a German accent. The show ended about the same time as the war ended--evidently Don and Red didn't have anything to do after the victory.

DOROTHY GORDON

One of the most outspoken of the advocates of "better radio for children" was Dorothy Gordon. She wrote a book entitled *All Children Listen,* an idealistic tome pointing out the importance of radio's influence on children. Unfortunately, one of her examples was how radio was used to influence children in Nazi Germany and in Russia (probably not a popular idea even in 1939), while in America, radio was used to sell bread.

Dorothy Gordon came to Mutual with her own program of stories and songs for 15 minutes, three times a week, in 1938. She had plenty of experience in children's radio, having served as musical director for the *American School of the Air* beginning in 1931. She was the only performer on the show, and wanted to prove that folk songs and children's classics could be as entertaining as the thrillers; certainly they would do more good for the kids. She was sponsored by Wheatena, and *Newsweek* in December of 1938 said the sponsor was cooperating "by not offering prizes and by omitting ballyhoo superlatives from commercial announcements" (p. 32). In spite of focusing on such stories as *Peter Pan, Alice in Wonderland* and *Pinocchio,* and in spite of being endorsed by the American Library Association, the Child Study Association, the United Parents Association, and the General Federation of Women's Clubs, *Dorothy Gordon* was on the air for only one season. Why the show failed isn't known; but a show of this kind going head-to-head with the thrillers (it was scheduled at 5:45 PM) was probably doomed from the beginning.

FLASH GORDON

The space hero *Flash Gordon* came from the pages of the comics (from the strip that was so beautifully drawn by Alex Raymond) and to the air over Mutual as a 15-minute serial in 1935. The show only lasted a couple of years, which seems odd, given the success of the comic strip and three movie serials, in 1936, 1938, and 1940. After all, *Buck Rogers* was on the air for a number of years, and Flash had everything that Buck did and more--a strange planet named Mongo, an evil ruler named Ming the Merciless, a mad scientist (Dr. Zarkoff), and a beautiful girl (Dale Arden) to help the handsome Flash. The tale began with Flash and Dale being kidnapped aboard the rocket ship of Hans Zarkoff, a crazed scientist who thought the planet Mongo was going to collide with Earth. Once they got to Mongo, however, Zarkoff conveniently regained his sanity in order to become one of Flash's comrades.

The episode of March 8, 1935, began with sound effects of a spaceship and the theme music. The announcer's voice is heard: "Presenting the amazing interplanetary adventures of *Flash Gordon!* (Music) These thrilling adventures come to you as they are pictured each Sunday in the *Comic Weekly,* the world's greatest pictorial supplement of humor and adventure. The *Comic Weekly,* now present in 32 tabloid-sized pages, each page in full four colors is distributed everywhere as an integral part of your Hearst Sunday papers. (Music comes up again) For the benefit of those who might not have heard the earlier episodes, here is the story to date. Flash Gordon,

internationally famous American athlete, his beautiful
sweetheart Dale Arden, and Dr. Zarkoff, a great scientist,
left the earth on a rocket ship. They crashed on the planet
Mongo and were captured by Ming the Merciless, the cruel
emperor of Mongo who commanded Dale Arden to marry
him, and ordered that Flash be killed. But Flash escaped
through the help of Emperor Ming's beautiful daughter
Aura who fell deeply in love with him and proposed
marriage. Flash refused, saying he loved Dale Arden.
Flash then met Thun, the powerful huge bearded Prince of
the Lion Men, and Prince Barin, the former member of
Emperor Ming's Court. Joined by Dr. Zarkoff, these four
friends plotted to overthrow the government of Emperor
Ming and rescue Dale Arden. They were almost
successful, but at the last moment, with victory practically
within their grasp, they were re-captured by Emperor
Ming's soldiers, and the four friends, together with Dale
Arden, were condemned to a fate worse than death.
Securely bound, they were placed on a gyroship and sent as
slaves to the prison city of Hawkmen. Now we continue
the story. (At last!) The prison ship carrying our friends
roared through the stratosphere, on the way to the prison
city of the Hawkmen. In the cell room, Flash and Prince
Thun worked feverishly on each other's bonds." Flash and
Thun free each other, and overpower the guard when he
comes to bring them food. They meet the other two outside
the door (they have also escaped their bonds), and the four
go to rescue Dale. Then Dr. Zarkoff asks to have a
valuable piece of scientific apparatus removed from the
ship, which apparently has landed (not heard by the
listeners). Zarkoff needs the great strength of Thun to
accomplish this task, so the other two run into the forest
nearby. Suddenly Zarkoff and Thun hear a rushing sound
overhead--it's the Hawkmen, who swoop down on them,

snatch them up and fly off toward the prison city of the
Hawkmen, while Dale and Flash and Barin watch in horror!
Barin says they'll never be seen again--no one has ever
escaped from the Hawkmen. Suddenly, they see a rocket
ship approaching--it lands!--(the sound effects resemble
something being sucked into a vacuum cleaner). The pilot
alights from the ship--it's Princess Aura! She gives Flash
one last chance, as he says, "I suppose you still want me to
marry you." Aura replies, "Yes--marry me and the Empire
ees yours, and your friends go free." "And if I refuse?"
"The Hawkmen will keel all of you. You shall never marry
theese earthgirl, Dale Arden!" Flash nobly makes his
choice--"My dear Princess, if I must make a choice, I
choose Dale and death!" Dale (equally noble) says she
doesn't care, as long as they are together. The Princess
leaves in her spaceship (whoosh) to get the Hawkmen.
Barin tells them that within the hour, every Hawkman on
the planet will be after them, and sure enough! They are
captured and taken before King Vultan, ruler of the
Hawkmen. He tells Aura that, according to the laws of
Mongo, she can have one of them, but the others belong to
him! Of course, Aura chooses "the yellow-haired youth."
Vultan has plans for Dale, but she cleverly asks the King to
spare Flash. "Just because I beg for his life doesn't mean
I'm in love with him--he is but a youth, but you, impressive
Majesty, are a man!" Vultan (who has a really nasty and
suggestively dirty laugh) is pleased, and plans to make her
his wife as soon as the high priest can be found. In the
meantime, Flash and the others are in the torture cells,
stoking the atomic furnaces of the Hawkmen. Zarkoff has
a plan--he has Flash wrap his manacles around a shovel,
and somehow the electric wire which is supposed to
electocute Flash if he tries anything sets off the radium.
Meanwhile, Dale and Vultan are waiting for the high priest.

Flash arrives in time to overpower Vultan, and with a blow that would kill an ordinary man, knocks him unconscious. But before Flash and Dale can escape, some unknown natural diaster occurs. The theme music begins and the announcer concludes, "What is happening to the city of Hawkmen, perched so precariously 5000 feet above the ground on the planet Mongo? What terrifying experience awaits our friends? Be sure to listen in again next week for the continuation of the amazing interplanetary adventures of *Flash Gordon,* same all-star American athlete who will appear in full color pictures next Sunday on the big 32-page comic supplement of your Hearst Sunday newspaper. What a treat is in store for you in next Sunday's *Comic Weekly,* where, besides *Flash Gordon,* you'll find the greatest array of funny people ever assembed in any magazine, waiting to entertain you." He names the comic strips, and invites us back for another adventure next week. The theme music comes up to end.

Like the other very early radio programs, much of the story was told by narration, rather than by dialogue and sound effects. The sound effects were sparse and not particularly realistic, and some of the voices were hard to tell apart. The acting was stiff and awkward, possibly because of the dialogue, which was hardly what one would call conversational. It was very difficult to tell where any of the characters were at any given time, because they seemed to disappear and re-appear without any explanatory dialogue or narration. None of these defects were overwhelmingly serious, however, for these faults were common to the other early radio dramas for children. Probably the cardinal sin committed by the writer was the emphasis on romance--which was a "no-no" on the Children's Hour. After all, a space serial such as this would have appealed primarily to the boys, with rocket ships and ray guns; but most young boys would have gagged on the romance. Possibly parents might have objected also; the story was full of "dirty old men" who would force the beautiful young Dale into an unwanted marriage. The format of the show was 15-minute serialized stories, with the usual cliffhanger ending. *Flash Gordon* was also seen on television in 1953, in a syndicated 30-minute program.

GENE AUTRY'S MELODY RANCH

Gene Autry, America's favorite singing cowboy, began his career on the radio in 1929, but soon moved to the Silver Screen, where he became a hero to the Saturday afternoon matinee crowd. Gene returned to radio in January of 1940 with his own show, which ran on CBS with Wrigley's Doublemint Gum as the sponsor until 1956. (It was running simultaneously with the television programs on CBS-TV from 1950 through 1956.) The show started out in a 15-minute slot on Sunday evenings, but was expanded to a 30-minute format later. The entire run was either on Saturday or Sunday evenings, reflecting Autry's popularity with adults as well as children. The show featured songs and a story of some adventure involving Autry and his pals, including Pat Buttram, his gravelly-voiced sidekick who provided the humor. There were a number of singing groups that appeared over the years, including the Cass County Boys, the Gene Autry Blue Jeans, the Pinafores, the Melody Ranch Six, the Johnny Bond Trio, and the King Sisters.

The first show, from January 7, 1940, began with the announcer speaking over background music: "Is there any one of us, who at some time or other in our lives, has not secretly pictured himself as a knight in shining armor, astride a powerful charger, thundering through adventure and hardships, to a romantic rescue? The American symbol of all these characters is the cowboy of our own Western plains and deserts who lives close to nature, relying more than any of us do today on himself alone and his ever-faithful horse. Our hero of Melody Ranch is Gene Autry, America's favorite singing cowboy, who is a symbol of the clean-thinking, honesty, and integrity of the American people. Gene has achieved success through his fine work in Republic Pictures. Millions of picture-goers know him and love him--much of his success is due to the fact that he, personally, lives the characters he depicts. Many of us can remember the many characters made famous by Horatio Alger. Gene Autry's own history is an Alger story, as you'll hear in a moment. But now, meet the boss of our imaginary Melody Ranch, Gene Autry!" The music comes up to finish. We are greeted by Autry, who says "howdy" to his fans and sings a song. The announcer returns to set the scene for a story about how Gene got his start. After working as a cowhand, he went to work in a train depot as a telegraph operator. His old partner, Tex, comes in to the depot and urges Gene to return to the range. They talk about life and how Gene wants more experience in other things. "But I ain't goin' back to the range till I'm sure I can meet any man on his own ground, so I'm lookin' the ground over." Tex asks how Champion (Autry's horse) feels about it. Just then, a stranger comes into the office and notices Autry's guitar--he asks Gene to sing a real Western song. He sings "Back in the Saddle Again" for the stranger, who advises Gene to go to New York and enter show business. The stranger leaves his wire to be sent, and Tex recognizes him as Will Rogers! After a commercial for Doublemint Gum, Autry winds up with some more folksy talk about how most of us would like to escape our troubles, and "sorta sink down around the campfire with the boys, and I hope that's what all you folks who've been here with us are going to do next Sunday evening." The announcer comes in to conclude: "Gene Autry, America's favorite singing cowboy, the square-shootin' lad who climbed to success the hard way, is going to be with us every Sunday evening, thanks to you local merchants who display and sell healthful, refreshing, delicious Doublemint Gum. Millions go to their favorite theaters to see Gene, and thrill to his singing in Republic Pictures. And now, Gene Autry comes to visit you, to sit around your firesides with you, swapping stories of the colorful West, telling you his adventures and singing you the grand songs we all love so well. Here is a new program, a program to carry you out of yourselves, out of this troubled world of ours, out into the great open plains of the West--a program that brings you color, American humor and American song by that successful interpreter of our nation's most tuneful folk songs, Gene Autry. So, join Gene and the boys of Melody Ranch next Sunday night and bring your family and friends along too, when Gene will be..." Guitar music comes up under his words, and then Gene sings "Back in the Saddle Again." The first program was not really typical of the series, but more of a promo for the show.

By 1948, the 30-minute version began with singing: "He's back in the saddle, again..." followed by the announcer: "Yes, it's time once again for *Melody Ranch* and Gene Autry!" Then Gene sings his theme song. "That's right, folks, it's another visit with all the gang here at Melody Ranch. There's Pat Buttram, the Cass County Boys, the Gene Autry Blue Jeans, Carl Cotner's Melody Ranch Hardway Six featuring Alvino Rey, and yours truly, Charlie Lyon. Right now, though, meet the boss man himself, America's favorite cowboy, Gene Autry!" Gene sings "Gimme That Old Time Religion." He greets the radio audience, and sings two more songs. After that, we hear a crash, and "It's me, Mister Artery." Pat Buttram tells Gene he's been working on his car. After a few jokes, the Cass County Boys sing, Gene sings two more songs, then: "You know, I get a lot of pleasure recalling the days when I was a kid--all the things I used to do. Maybe it's 'cause I'm one of those fellows that memories mean a lot to. Anyway, it was those same memories about one of the finest people I've ever known that reminded me of today's story. Some years ago, I was sittin' at my office desk one morning goin' over business details, when Johnny Bond walked in." Johnny brings in the mail, which includes a letter from Nell Johnson, his teacher, who last saw Gene when he was 12 years old. A few months later, Gene goes to visit her. But before he leaves town, he drops by the local bank to visit an old schoolmate, Dave Phillips, who is the banker. Phillips tells Gene that Miss Nell's property will be auctioned in a couple of days. Gene changes his mind about leaving, and he calls some of his other old schoolmates to gather them in the town for the auction. They raise the money, $4000, to buy her property. Gene tells Phillips to close the bidding at $4000. The men then tell Miss Nell that they bought the property so they'd have a place to meet each year, and they are putting her in charge of it. After the story, Gene sings. Then we hear the theme song and the announcer: "Next week at this same time, Gene Autry and all the gang at Melody Ranch will be heard over these same stations. This is Charlie Lyon, inviting you to be tuned our way."

Though the program consisted mostly of songs by Autry and the various singing groups, the stories were designed for the youngsters and were full of old-fashioned American values and the code of the Old West. The jokes told by Pat were easily understood by the kids, and a youngster could hear his movie idol talking, it seemed, just to him! The shows had something that appealed to the whole family.

THE GREEN HORNET

A masked avenger who worked outside the law, *The Green Hornet* was one of the creations of George W. Trendle of WXYZ in Detroit along with *The Lone Ranger*. The scripts were written by Fran Striker, who also wrote *The Lone Ranger,* so it might come as no surprise that these masked men were related. Britt Reid, young and dashing newspaper publisher, was the Green Hornet and the son of Dan Reid, nephew of the Lone Ranger! Other similarities, besides the mask, included the faithful sidekick, the only man who knew the Hornet's true identity; Tonto's Asian counterpart, Kato. Kato started out to be Japanese, but when the United States joined World War II, he became Filipino. And, instead of the great horse Silver, the Green Hornet had the sleek, superpowered car--the streamlined Black Beauty. Both heroes operated outside the law and sometimes were the target of police or sheriffs. Another similarity was the use of classical music for the theme, something Trendle did because the music was public domain, and therefore cut production costs. Neither the Lone Ranger or the Green Hornet ever shot to kill, and they always left calling cards (the silver bullet and the hornet).

After starting on WXYZ in 1936, the show went to Mutual in 1938, then to NBC Blue in 1939. It was one of the few early "thrillers" that was a complete story, told in 30 minutes. Although *The Green Hornet* was designed primarily for children, it was scheduled at 8 PM for its first few years, before moving to Saturdays, and then closer to the Children's Hour. There was also a *Green Hornet* comic strip and movie serials in 1939 and 1944, but these came after the radio show, rather than preceding it, as did so many others.

One of the earlier episodes, broadcast October 31, 1939, opened with the familiar sound of the hornet: "Bzzzzzzz! He hunts the biggest of all game--public enemies that even the G-Men cannot reach--*The Green Hornet!*" The music, "Flight of the Bumble-Bee," playing for 55 seconds, was very well established. "With his faithful valet Kato, Britt Reid, daring young publisher, matches wits with the underworld, risking his life that criminals and racketeers within the law may feel its weight, by the sting of the Green Hornet! (Sound effects: car) Ride with Britt Reid, as he races toward another thrilling adventure--the Green Hornet Strikes again." (Car sound up, then we hear the Hornet's voice) "Hurry, Kato! We're out to smash a parking lot racket!" (Bzzzzzz fades out) Next was one of the more unusual and creative bits of scripting, a montage of sound effects and voices, depicting the thugs demanding protection money from parking lot owners. A woman's voice, counting money, continues in the background, with music, and dialogue: "They won't listen to reason--smash a few of the cars, throw a couple o' bombs, start a few fires--they'll lay it on the line! Here's the parking lot--toss that bomb! There she goes! (Sound effects: explosion) Ten percent? I'll pay!" Then we join Britt and Irishman Mike Axford, as they attempt to park a car in a lot owned by a man named Sheaffer. The lot is virtually empty, and the owner tries to dissuade them, because of things that have been happening to cars parked there. Then inside the *Daily Sentinel,* reporter Lenore Case receives a letter from the Green Hornet, saying he's

going to take over the parking lot racket. It turns out
Sheaffer also got a letter from the Hornet, and now we're
all set for a battle between the racketeer Bleeker and the
Hornet! Britt Reid returns to his apartment and Kato, "the
only living man to know him as the Green Hornet!" By
now, of course, the *Sentinel* is out on the streets ("Extra,
extra! Read all about it!") with the two letters printed, so
Reid tells Kato to get the car and the gas gun and be ready
for Bleeker! They watch the parking lot, and see the crooks
arrive. One of them hits the cop guarding the lot over the
head, knocking him out. The Hornet then calls the lot, and
talks to Bleeker who answers the phone, pretending to be
the owner. He agrees to pay the Hornet, at midnight
tomorrow. Of course the Green Hornet arrives early,
gasses Sheaffer with the gas gun (but just enough so that
he'll wake up at midnight), and changes the window shade
in the parking lot building to one with a paper cut-out of the
Green Hornet. "The Green Hornet'll be here at midnight,
Kato, but not in person." Bleeker and the boys arrive, see
the silhouette of the Hornet and shoot at it. Just about that
time the cops arrive and get the crooks. "Read all about
it--Green Hornet still at large!" Then another 50 seconds of
"The Flight of the Bumble Bee," followed by, "The story
you have just heard is a copyrighted feature of *The Green
Hornet, Incorporated.* The situations and characters
depicted in the drama are fictitious. Any similarity to
actual persons or events of the past or present is
coincidental." (Music up and out)

A later episode, broadcast in late 1946 or early
1947, had a different introduction (reportedly because of
the objections of J. Edgar Hoover to the reference to
G-Men) (Dunning, 1976, p. 254). "Bzzzzzzzz---He hunts
the biggest of all game--public enemies who try to destroy
our America! The theme music, now shortened to 20

seconds, is followed by the remainder of the introduction.
". . . ride with Britt Reid in the thrilling adventure, 'The
Hornet Does It!' The Green Hornet strikes again!
Bzzzzzzzz---" After Jack Kenley is released from state
prison, his old confederates pick him up. Although Kenley
wants to go straight, they threaten him and he rejoins them,
as the crooks hijack first a boatload, then a truckload, of
sugar, by posing as cops. The reason for hijacking sugar
(giving the clue as to when the episode was broadcast) was
that sugar was one of the few things still rationed. Mike
Axford, the Irishman, who is the police reporter for the
Sentinel, calls city editor Gunnigan and tells him of the
first hijacking. "Then the hijackers got away with the load
of sugar, huh?" Mike replies, "What d'ya think they did, sit
out there in the middle of the river and make themselves
some fudge? Of course they got away with the sugar!"
(Mike, who plays the stereotyped dumb Irishman, is given
to such smart-aleck remarks.) In the second hijacking, the
crooks leave the seal of the Green Hornet on the
truck-driver's forehead (he was hit over the head and
knocked out, naturally). The indignant Hornet sends one of
his infamous letters to the Sarge, "I don't like being blamed
for things I don't do!" In the meantime, Jack has decided to
go to the cops, and (brilliantly), the Green Hornet has
predicted this would happen, now that the crooks know the
Hornet AND the cops are after them. Stepping through a
secret panel in the rear of the closet in the bedroom, Britt
Reid and Kato go through a secret passageway to an
abandoned adjoining building, where the sleek,
superpowered Black Beauty, the streamlined car of the
Green Hornet, is parked. They go to police headquarters,
park and wait for a man "who seems nervous--who
hesitates about going in." When Jack arrives, so do the
other crooks, who shoot at him. They are gassed by the

Green Hornet, and arrested. Jack, of course, will get off light. "The Hornet's done it again!" The ending has changed somewhat, with the theme music shortened, and: "These popular radio dramas, created by George W. Trendle, are a copyrighted feature of *The Green Hornet, Incorporated.* All characters, names, places and incidents used are fictitious." (Music up to end)

Although there was plenty of violence in the episodes, no one was actually killed. The gas gun was the modern day counterpart of the Lone Ranger's habit of shooting the gun out of the bad guy's hand. The scripting and dialogue were higher quality than many of the other children's shows (typical of Fran Striker's writing). Sound effects were plentiful and realistic (a real automobile door was mounted permanently in a sound studio at WXYZ for the sound of Black Beauty's door opening and closing) (Osgood, 1981, p. 167). The newspaper setting added other characters, such as reporters Lenore Case, Mike Axford, and Ed Lowry, and Gunnigan, the editor, who provided the explanatory dialogue that carried the story line, rather than relying on narration by the announcer. In its last years, the show was on twice a week during the Children's Hour, and it ended in 1952. *The Green Hornet* returned, this time on television, in 1966 through 1967.

HOOFBEATS

Typical of 1930's movie fare were the Class B Westerns, low budget formula films featuring a cowboy hero who was hard riding and hard fighting; a hero who knew right from wrong and always prevailed over the bad guys of the Old West. Such a hero was Buck Jones, "America's most famous cowboy." (Similar claims were made by most of the cowboy stars.) Buck came to radio for a short time in 1937 with *Hoofbeats,* a 15-minute syndicated show starring Buck himself. This was one of the few Westerns in which the hero had no sidekick to help him vanquish the enemies of the West (and consequently, no one to carry on conversations with on a regular basis).

One of the episodes of *Hoofbeats* began with the show's regular announcer, identified only as "The Old Wrangler." After the theme music was established, we hear, "*Hoofbeats!* Howdy, folks! The makers of Grape Nuts Flakes, America's most famous cereal in flake form, again bring you America's most famous cowboy, Buck Jones, in *Hoofbeats!* All you boys and girls have seen Buck and his horse Silver in his thrillin', red-blooded movin' pictures, crammed with action and excitement. Well, that's the kind of story this radio series is too, and I hope you'll stick with us 'cause I know you're gonna like it a lot. And here's something else your're gonna like a lot..." A commercial for Grape Nuts Flakes follows. The theme music comes up and under, "In our last episode, the Dagger Hilt outfit was driving the herd into the box canyon, before the storm, and they knew they were being followed by men who meant them no good. Buck Jones has joined up with the Dagger Hilt crowd, because he's looking for three men on whom he has sworn revenge. One of them bears the mark of a dagger hilt on his shoulder. One of the men, Red River, knows that the boss of the Dagger Hilt, Gore, has the sinister mark on his shoulder, but he doesn't tell Buck. Instead, he urges him to leave, for even though they've been friendly, Red River has to stick with the outfit." The sound effects of hoofbeats comes in and under. Gore and Red are talking about getting rid of Buck and a kid that's been following them, because they have the boy's cow. The men think the kid is a jinx. Red urges Buck to leave, and they hear thunder. They are driving the herd to the

canyon, when they drive through the camp of a pretty girl
and her old-timer father. Buck and Red go to apologize for
driving through their camp, and to get a drink of water.
The girl admires Buck's horse. Later, the girl comes to
their camp with the young boy and demands they give him
his cow. Buck says he will get the cow, and the boss, Gore,
objects. There is a fight--Buck sees the mark of the Dagger
Hilt on Gore--gunshots ring out, and a stampede begins!
The theme music comes up, and the Old Wrangler
concludes the day's episode: "So Buck has found one of the
men he wanted--Gore! Did Buck get him? Or did the wild
stampede sweep Gore before it? We'll learn the answers
when we meet again! But in the meantime, here's a tip for
you, straight from the shoulder, too." A Grape Nuts Flakes
commercial follows, "mighty good chuck." Buck returns to
tell about his club, "The Buck Jones Club." The kids can
get a membership badge and some prizes; one is a cowboy
hat like Buck wears (the prizes may be obtained by sending
in a Grape Nuts Flakes boxtop, of course). The Old
Wrangler concludes over the sound of hoofbeats: "And so
Buck Jones rides away once again, but your trails will cross
soon. Why not do as Buck suggests, and join up with his
club? Just send your name and address with one red top
from a box of Grape Nuts Flakes to Buck Jones, in care of
this station. This offer is good in the United States, only,
and you'll get your membership badge. So, till next
thrillin' episode of *Hoofbeats,* this is your friend, the Old
Wrangler." The theme music comes up to close.

     Dunning (1976) calls the show a classic of juvenile
radio and characteristic of the productions of the 1930's (p.
287). There was certainly plenty of action and sound
effects and voices that sounded like the characters they
played. There was a genuine Western cowboy star, some
bad guys, a pretty girl (but no romance); all of the

ingredients for a successful Children's Hour Western. The mystery is why the run of *Hoofbeats* was so short. MacDonald (1979) believed it was because of the lack of a sidekick for Buck, and therefore an inability to generate any humor (p. 198).

HOP HARRIGAN

Aviators were very popular among the younger set during World War II, perhaps even more than before the war. Joining the other daredevil pilots on the radio, *Hop Harrigan* came from *All-American Comics* to the Blue Network in 1942 with a 15-minute serial. It was followed by a movie serial in 1946. Hop and his sidekick mechanic Tank Tinker and girlfriend Gale Nolan never quite enjoyed the following of Captain Midnight, but they did have a six-year run, from 1942 until 1948 (the last two years on Mutual) when the popularity of war stories and battles with saboteurs was waning.

The episode labeled September 17, 1943, began with the announcer: "Presenting *Hop Harrigan,* America's Ace of the Airways!" Next we hear Hop's plane, then Hop asking for clearance, "CX-4, calling control tower, CX-4 calling control tower, standing by!" Then the filtered voice of the control tower, "Control tower back to CX-4--wind southeast, ceiling twelve hundred. Alllll clear. . ." Hop cries, "Okayyy---this is Hop Harrigan, coming innnnn!" (Sound effects: airplane) "Yes, it's America's Ace of the Airways, coming in for another transcribed episode in the adventures of *Hop Harrigan!*" Then the announcer, Glenn Riggs, describes the landing gear on the B-36 bomber, "the world's biggest" bomber. "And now, to our story. With the startling revelation that Bill King was the man who whistled, and who had caused the temporary disappearance

of Tank Tinker, the mystery of the vanishing men came to
an abrupt and surprising end. As we continue now, it is
early the following morning. Hop and Tank, resuming
active operation of their airport at Lakeville, are flying a
cargo run to New City. With only a moderate load in the
Beechcraft, Gale's come along, and as they skim through
the clear morning air, they discuss the events of the
preceding week." Hop and Gale and Tank are talking (with
the sound of the plane in the background) about Bill King
and the mystery they have just solved. King, who "has a
screw loose," will likely be committed to a mental
institution. Hop talks to the tower at New City, who gives
him permission to land. But a DC-4 is coming in too fast
on their right! The tower tells the pilot to pull up and go
around, but the DC-4 keeps coming in! Hop has to pull his
plane off on the grass, and the bigger plane barely misses
them! When it comes to a stop, the pilot jumps to the
ground, not waiting for a ladder, and runs, his face white!
Hop and Tank pursue him, and when they catch him, he is
terrified. "Let go of me! The Jap, he's comin' after
me--he's gonna get me! Hop tries to calm him--"There's
nobody after you!" "I saw him--the Zero's after me! I shot
him down, and now he's comin' back--he wants to take me
with him! Let go!" The announcer returns with more stories
of the big bomber, which will carry its own drone
radio-controlled fighter planes inside. "Fellows and girls,
whether it's a B-36 or a Piper Cub, it's fun to fly! And
always remember, America needs flyers!" Then he brings
us up to date and we return to the action. Hop has to knock
the pilot out to calm him down, and the other pilot from the
DC-4 arrives and tells them he'll take care of it. He's
somewhat rude, and Gale says they should go with the
unconscious pilot, because the boy needs medical attention.
The announcer returns: "But as Hop looks back at the still

figure stretched out on the ground, and at the other pilot, bending over him, he doesn't realize that he soon will know what happened--that he and Tank are to become involved in a weird and terrifying mystery of the airlanes. So don't miss episode number two of 'The Riddle of the Ghostly Avenger!' (Sound effects: plane starting up) "Tune in and fly with *Hop Harrigan,* America's Ace of the Airways! (Sound effects: plane taking off) So long, Hop! We'll be seeing you same time, same Mutual station! *Hop Harrigan* is a transcribed, copyrighted feature appearing in *All-American Comic Magazine.*" (plane sound up to close).

Although the episode is dated 1943, the likelihood is that it actually ran in 1947 or 1948, when the program was on Mutual. Also, the story line has more of a post-war theme: the ex-fighter pilot who has shot down Japs and is now flying a cargo plane back home. This was one of the better programs, with plenty of realistic conversation between Hop and the control tower, lots of sound effects and action, and an unsolved mystery, sure to keep the kids coming back to find out more! The show was mostly sustaining, so the times where commercials would have run were filled by educational tidbits about planes and aviation. The show followed the 15-minute serial format for its entire run, even when many of the other shows were adopting the 30-minute format.

HOPALONG CASSIDY

Many of the inhabitants of the Children's Hour came there from the comics or from the movies, and some moved on to television. But *Hopalong Cassidy* stands alone as the only Western hero to go from the pages of a series of Western stories written by Clarence Mulford, to the movies, then to television in 1949, then to a comic strip, and last--to radio! The show was quite late in appearing on the scene--by the time of the first broadcast on Mutual in 1950, television was off with a bang, and the decline of radio drama was under way. The one and only Hopalong was, of course, William Boyd. Boyd had acquired the rights to all the old *Hopalong Cassidy* films, just in time to sell them to television, where they were an instant success (Dunning, 1976, p. 290). Hopalong was the typical "good guy" of the radio West--no smoking, drinking, cussing, or women. Just as most of the other Western heroes, Hoppy had a sidekick, the crusty old-timer California Carlson. The shows were 30-minute complete stories, and soon moved to CBS.

In the episode entitled "The Songbird of Santa Fe," we hear the theme music first, followed by the announcer: "With action and suspense, out of the Old West comes the most famous hero of them all, *Hopalong Cassidy* --starring William Boyd! (Theme music comes up) The ring of the silver spurs heralds the most amazing man ever to ride the prairies of the early West, Hopalong Cassidy. The same Hoppy you cheer in motion pictures and the same California you've laughed at a million times. Raw courage and quick shooting have built a legend around this famous hero. Hopalong is a name to be feared, respected and admired, for this great cowboy rides the trails of adventure and excitement. William Boyd as Hopalong Cassidy and Andy Clyde as California. What's our story this time, Hoppy?" Hoppy comes in to set the scene for "The Songbird of Santa Fe." Hoppy and California have arrived in Santa Fe just as a festival is beginning, but they have come to keep a promise to a dead man. Next we hear two men talking about Hoppy's arrival. Apparently there is a ring involved, and the two (obviously criminals) are after it. Next, Hoppy and California are at the bar of the Grand

Hotel--but no alcohol for our heroes--they are drinking sarsaparilla. Hoppy tells California he'll feel better in the morning because of it. A stagecoach arrives, and a beautiful girl gets off. A man tells them she's Lorraine LaCher, a famous singer from Paris who has come to sing at the Opera House. California shows off his tomahawk throwing abilities by throwing one at the post the man was leaning against, and we hear the crowd muttering in the background about the tomahawk. Hoppy goes to deliver the ring; naturally the two crooks are waiting for him. The man called Destral tells his henchman, "Stand out on the balcony. If I say, 'Stranger, you're makin' a mistake,' pump lead into him." Hoppy is looking for a man named Mack Kiley to give him the ring that a jeweler in Las Cruces asked him to deliver. The jeweler had been badly wounded and died. Destral pretends to be Kiley, but Hoppy is suspicious. "If your name is Kiley, why would you have the initials 'A.D.' on your belt buckle?" Destral says it had belonged to a friend, but Hopalong is not satisfied, and says he will keep the ring for a while. Destral gives his henchman the cue, but Hoppy shoots first. "Next time, have your gunmen watch their shadows--especially in the late afternoon sun." In the meantime, California has located Kiley, who is making a speech at the hotel. Kiley came to Santa Fe as a bricklayer, and after becoming a success, built the Opera House. He had ordered the ring as a gift for Miss LaCher. Suddenly, they are set upon by four thugs, but Kiley, California and Hoppy fight them off. Hopalong believes the diamond ring brings nothing but violence and death. The next morning, he is awakened by the Deputy Sheriff, who asks him to identify a tomahawk as the one belonging to California. It was found across the hall, next to the dead body of Lorraine LaCher! California is nowhere to be found, and the Sheriff thinks he is responsible for the singer's death. Hoppy talks to Kiley, who tells him he and Miss LaCher were engaged to be married. He had given her the ring the night before, and he wants it back--not just because it cost $10,000, but for the sentimental value as well. Kiley believes Ace Destral is responsible--Ace is a gambler who has a grudge against Kiley. They go to the inquest, where a man tells them he thinks he knows where California is--"holed up in a shack just outside of town." Hoppy goes there and rescues California who has been shanghaied by one of Destral's henchmen. They return to Kiley's office with the Sheriff, and the surprise solution to the murder is revealed--Kiley is the murderer! Lorraine had refused to marry him, and he hit her with a brick hammer and tried to frame California. Suddenly Destral, who has been in cahoots with Kiley all along, comes in with his guns drawn. But he wants to prove he is the fastest gun, so he holsters his gun and he and Hoppy shoot it out. The Sheriff, who was wounded in the shoulder by Destral, asks if he's finished. California replies, "He shore is--deader'n a side of beef!" Kiley wants to know how Hoppy figured it out. It seems Hoppy caught him lying at the inquest about the time that he left the hotel. Kiley said the clerk saw him leave, but that particular clerk wasn't on duty until later. The announcer tells us about the next episode, and the theme music comes up. He concludes with, "*Hopalong Cassidy,* starring William Boyd, is transcribed and produced in the West by Walter White, Jr. 'Songbird of Santa Fe' was written by Buckley Angel, with original music under the personal direction of Albert Glasser. All stories are based upon the characters created by Clarence E. Mulford. This is a Commodore Production."

     The show reflects the increased sophistication of scripting and sound effects typical of the later years of the radio drama. The actors all have the proper voices that sound like they belong to the characters. The action is carried by dialogue and sound effects, rather than narration, and the story line is fairly plausible and easy for the young listeners to follow. There is plenty of action, mystery, a few dead bodies, and justice prevails--all the right ingredients for success. But Hopalong and his pal were already on television, and as more kids had access to the small screen, the listening audience diminished. The radio show ended in 1952, one year after the television run had ended.

JACK ARMSTRONG,
THE ALL-AMERICAN BOY

One of the earliest and longest-running residents of the Children's Hour was the indomitable *Jack Armstrong,* hero of Hudson High and another of the adventuresome schoolboys. Jack and his cousins Betty and Billy Fairfield arrived on CBS in 1933. Early shows dealt with Jack's adventures at good old Hudson High, where the opposing teams reportedly used questionable tactics (Egad!) to win (Eisenberg, 1936, pp. 208-209). Of course that sort of thing wasn't condoned in the early days of children's programming. Soon Jack, Billy and Betty left Hudson High to take up world-traveling adventure with Uncle Jim Fairfield, inventor, who owned an aircraft factory. Just exactly how these three adolescents got by with playing hooky for years was not really explained. Supposedly, they were to take along their books and keep up with studies, but this was never part of the daily scripts. The show ran as a 15-minute serial for most of the run, moving to NBC Blue in 1936.

A 1935 episode begins with sounds of cheering:

"Rah, rah, rah! Jack Armstrong! Jack Armstrong! Ya-aaay!" The announcer informs us, "*Jack Armstrong, the All American Boy* is on the air--in person--to get you to eat Wheaties! Fellows, girls--hang on for thrills, excitement, adventure! Today, Wheaties bring you a story of champions in action!" (Sound effects: crowd cheering). Next, a Max Carey of the Amateur Baseball Union talks about the Wheaties All-American team that won the World Championship in Japan. He talks about the trip and the tournament. "Thanks a lot, Max Carey, you were swell. Now, *Jack Armstrong, the All-American Boy.* Yesterday after the *Pelican* caught fire, Jack offered to take a line across the packed ice floes so that Captain Hands and his men might be rescued. Here we are on deck. Jack has just started across. Listen!" Following is a long and tedious dialogue between several unidentified voices about the line and the equipment and whether or not Jack will make it to the *Pelican.* They are watching through binoculars and commenting on the fire aboard the *Pelican,* the whereabouts of its crew, and Jack's progress, and the fact that no one other than Jack could possibly attempt such a feat. After a discussion of how hard it is to see Jack, we have the impression he's traveled quite a distance, until we're told Jack's not more than 50 or 60 yards away. They lose sight of Jack, and Billy is ready to go to help, but we hear Jack's faint shouts. He must jump across some open water carrying the heavy line. After he jumps, he has to cross a section of thin ice. Jack finally makes it to the ship--Captain Hands is helping him aboard! "So Jack reaches the *Pelican* safely at last. But will there be time to rescue Captain Hands and the crew? Be sure to listen at this same time tomorrow evening to find out what happens next!" A Wheaties commercial follows.

With such slow-moving action, it seems amazing

the show was so popular. Because the scripts were written by a number of different writers, it is not known whether or not this particular episode was written by the creator of *Jack Armstrong,* Robert Hardy Andréws. In any case, the episode broadcast October 3, 1940, showed vast improvement in scripting. The opening had changed to the more familiar and long-lasting, "Jack Armstrong! Jack Armstrong! Jack Armstrong!" (done with an echo effect). Then the announcer, "*Jack Armstrong--the Allll---American Boy!*" Following is the familiar song: "Wave the flag for Hudson High, boys! Show them how we stand; Ever shall our team be champions known throughout the land! Hmmmmmmm (fading under) Wheaties, Breakfast of Champions, bring you the thrilling adventures of *Jack Armstrong, the All-American Boy.*" After the Wheaties commercial (a dialogue between two boys), "And now, *Jack Armstrong, the All-American Boy!* Uncle Jim's high-altitude amphibian is winging its silver way westward, high above the Sierra Nevada mountains, and the mighty Pacific is rolling up on the horizon. Uncle Jim is at the controls, and Jack and Billy and Betty are peering out through the windows of the sealed cabin, trying to spot the Golden Gate of San Francisco Harbor. In that harbor lies the small ship that will take them westward to the Philippines and to the Sulu Sea in search of a wrecked yacht with its treasure of rare uranium metal which Uncle Jim needs in his atom-splitting experiments. Listen!" They spot San Francisco Harbor, and Uncle Jim tells them about the Golden Gate Bridge, the "longest suspension bridge in the world." The plane starts down and Jack is put in charge of the supercharger that pressurizes the plane's interior; to "keep her at normal atmospheric pressure all the way down." Jack explains to Billy and Betty that this is a sub-stratosphere ship, traveling high (at 30,000 feet) where there isn't much air resistance, enabling them to travel across half the continent in just a few hours. The story gradually unfolds: it seems Black Beard tried to steal Uncle Jim's papers. "If that gang got ahold of the uranium--why, it might be all they need to split the atom before our scientists did it. Other people would have airplanes and rocket ships that would make this ship look like a toy." The plane dives for the Golden Gate; Betty squeals, "The bottom's falling out of my stomach!" They see the Spindrift, a two-master, the small yacht that will carry them to the Sulu Sea. But look! Someone is heading for the Spindrift in a skiff. Jack looks through the binoculars, and tells the others the man looks like a foreigner--like a mixture of different countries, "definitely not an American!" (The binoculars certainly must have been powerful.) This worries Uncle Jim, who tells Jack and Billy to hop a taxi as soon as they land and head to the yacht club where the boat is moored and find out what the chap's up to, and what he's doing aboard. "Watch out for rough stuff. This gang knows a thing or two in the manhandling game. I happen to know that one of this gang is an expert in jiujitsu." Jack and Billy are taken ashore from the seaplane, where Betty stays behind with Uncle Jim. They arrive at the yacht club, and find the Spindrift's skiff at the dock, and the mysterious skiff is tied up to the boat. They row out quietly, hoping to surprise the intruder. How are they going to keep this man aboard without resorting to "rough stuff," against Uncle Jim's wishes? Jack has an idea--they'll tie up alongside and throw the oars for both skiffs overboard. Then no one can leave until Uncle Jim gets there! "Now what? Do you think the mysterious prowler did hear Jack and Billy? And what is he doing on the Spindrift? You can bet he's up to no good, or Uncle Jim wouldn't be so worried about him. And when he finds he can't get back to shore before Uncle Jim arrives, the fur will be flying. So listen in, all of you this same time tomorrow to see what happens in the new and thrilling adventure--when--the strange visitor comes face-to-face with *Jack Armstrong---the Alllll---American Boy!*" The Wheaties commercial concludes with the jingle, "Have you trii--ed Wheaties; they're whole wheat with all of the bran. Won't you try Wheaties, for wheat is the best food of man....(fade) This is Franklin McCormick saying goodbye until tomorrow for General Mills, maker of Wheaties, Breakfast of Champions, who have just presented another episode of *Jack Armstrong, the All-American Boy*." The show concludes with the "Wave the flag for Hudson High" song.

Somewhere in the five years between the two episodes, the formula was found that made *Jack Armstrong* so successful. Exciting narration before and after the actual episode, enough action to keep the story moving, enough factual information that the young audience always learned something, futuristic gadgets, edge-of-the-chair cliffhanger endings, and frequent naming of the characters so that you *always* knew who was speaking, even if you didn't recognize the voice. Frequently the naming was overdone, but nonetheless, it worked. Stedman (1971) attributed the first name clutter to a script supervisor at the advertising agency, Blackett, Sample and Hummert (p. 189). The locales for the stories were always exotic--deepest Africa, the South Seas--nowhere on Earth was too far for the foursome to fight criminals, and the Axis during the war. The lone female character, Betty, had the usual tasks of girls in the world of juvenile radio--stay behind as much as possible, but get into terrible danger occasionally, necessitating rescue by the hero.

A *National Education Association Journal* critic

described Jack as "a holier-than-thou lad whom one would like to give a healthy sock in the eye just as a matter of principle" (Henry, 1935, p. 145). But not all agreed. *Newsweek* said that Jack had survived the perils of over 2,200 broadcasts, fighting mad bull elephants, pirates and Nazis--all without being a superboy with bulging muscles and X-ray vision. Jack's standards were ensured by Dr. Martin L. Reymert of the Mooseheart Laboratory of Childhood Research at Mooseheart, Illinois. As a script consultant, he insisted on a plot that was fairly plausible, good grammar, and no profanity, brutal murder, torture or kidnapping ("Jack, the Nazi killer," 1943, p. 80). Fair play and love of country were the themes. During World War II, more than a million children were members of Jack Armstrong's Write-a-Fighter Corps, whose members pledged to write one letter each month to a member of the Armed Forces. Premiums were a big part of the show's popularity, too--pedometers, torpedo flashlights, games, telescopes, guns, the Jack Armstrong Secret Whistle Ring, all "just like Jack's" and designed to boost the sale of Wheaties.

In 1947, Jack finally made it into the movies as the hero of a serial, as the popularity of the radio programs was diminishing. In 1947 the show became a 30-minute serial and in 1948 the complete-in-one episode format was adopted. Jack held on a little while longer by growing up and becoming *Armstrong of the S.B.I.* in 1950, a thinly disguised clone of *The F.B.I.* But the All-American boy didn't gain a following as an adult, and the show left the air in 1951.

JUNGLE JIM

Another serial featuring exotic locales and airplanes

was *Jungle Jim*. The name itself conjured up visions of lions and tigers and savages. The hero, Jungle Jim Bradley, originated in the comic strip drawn by Alex Raymond, who also created *Flash Gordon*. *Jungle Jim* made his way from the comic pages to a movie serial in 1937, and then to radio sometime in the early 1940's--the exact dates are unknown. *Jungle Jim* was also a syndicated television program in 1955, which starred Johnny Weismuller as the hero. Jim also had a faithful companion, the native Kolu, and a girlfriend, Shanghai Lil.

The show (an undated episode) opened with the sound of a storm, and the classical music theme. The announcer says, "Presenting the adventures of *Jungle Jim*! Last week, the Reverend Chalmers made an attempt to find out what was going on inside the mysterious cabin 307. The Reverend hoped Lin Foo would invite him and his daughter to take tiffin (an obsolete British name for lunch), but the wily Chinese excused himself after being introduced, and instead of writing letters as he said he was going to do, attempted to communicate with the Purple Triangle headquarters by radio. Meanwhile, the American Consul asked Jungle Jim to capture Derrick Bluger, a renegade American and head of the Purple Triangle Gang. The thrilling adventures of Jungle Jim are featured each Sunday in the *Comic Weekly,* the world's greatest pictorial supplement of humor and adventure. The *Comic Weekly,* each page printed in full color, is distributed everywhere as an integral part of your Hearst Sunday newspaper. And now, we continue our story. On the steamer bound for Shanghai, we find Lin Foo and his servant trying to establish radio contact with the Purple Triangle headquarters." Lin Foo's servant is trying to call headquarters, but he is unsuccessful--he suggests that perhaps they have been captured? Lin Foo thinks that isn't possible--he believes that Jungle Jim Bradley is the only one brilliant enough to do that, and he is supposed to be dead! What will they do? If they can't reach headquarters, they will have no orders when they reach Shanghai! Meanwhile, the missionary and his daughter are outside, keeping their eyes on cabin 307 where Lin Foo is. They are wondering if Jungle Jim is still alive, and how they are going to get in cabin 307 to find out what Lin Foo is up to. Then the Reverend has an idea! They go to their cabin and send for the Purser. They ask him to change their cabin to 308 (for the view). He asks about the door between 307 and 308, and finds out the lock is in 308. "If we can get moved into 308 without the Chinese knowing who their neighbors are, it won't be long before we know what the mysterious Lin Foo is being so mysterious about!" Then the announcer shifts the scene to the airport, where Jungle Jim finds his sidekick Kolu guarding Lil's plane. Jim asks where Shanghai Lil is--Kolu tells him she went to the hotel. Jim is surprised: "But I thought she was going to stay here and tune up our motor until I came back." Kolu replies, "White missy see man she no want meet--white missy run." Jim is incredulous--"Lil ran away from a man?" Jim says he will ask the airport manager to put the plane in a hangar, when someone calls him--according to Kolu, a "yellow-face." The Chinese introduces himself as Chung, the expedition guide sent to Jim by the American Consul. Chung advises Jim that they should get started as soon as possible--that night. Jim tells Kolu to take their things to the train--"I've got a little something to settle before I leave Shanghai." The announcer explains: "Before setting out on his dangerous mission to nip a budding revolution, Jim stops to bid farewell to Lilly DeVille." Lil tells Jim she'll miss him, and that she loves him. Jim wants her to clear up the mystery about herself. Lil was once in love with a powerful man, who sent her to Malaysia to pretend she was a goddess and steal the natives' gold. This is where Jim and Lil met, and it changed her life--Jim is so fine and noble, it made her despise herself! And--the man wanted the gold to help bring China under the rule of the Purple Triangle Gang. Jim is astounded--"Well, I'll be doggoned!" That's the man he's been assigned to capture--Derrick Bluger! Lil tells him to be careful--Derrick is a killer! Lil asks Jim to kiss her goodbye. Jim says, "Not goodbye, but au revoir." Next Jim, Kolu and Chung are on the northbound train discussing the plans. Chung alone knows where the Purple Triangle Gang is, and where to pick up the trail of Derrick Bluger! The announcer concludes the day's episode: "Now for the big adventure of the Purple Triangle headquarters and the trail of Derrick Bluger. The dramatization of the adventures of *Jungle Jim* you have just heard was based on incidents appearing in the *Comic Weekly*--the big *Comic Weekly* distributed with your Hearst Sunday newspaper everywhere. In the *Comic Weekly,* the world's greatest supplement of humor and adventure, you will find a feature called "Heroes of American History," that picturizes in full color the careers of great men and women and the story of our country. There are also all the famous characters who live in the world of color pictures, including *Skippy, Sentinel Louie, Bringing Up Father, Barney Google,* and the *Katzenjammer Kids.* Don't forget our date, next week, same time, same station for a continuation of the adventures of *Jungle Jim.*" The theme music comes up to close.

Although Terrace (1981) dates the show in the early 1940's, this *Jungle Jim* episode has the sound of the radio dramas of the middle 1930's: the involved, difficult to follow plot, the sparse and poorly done sound effects, the stilted dialogue, the emphasis on love and romance that the writers of children's programs had pretty much learned to avoid by the 1940's. The characters' voices sound quite similar to those in the *Flash Gordon* episode. (A coincidence?) The Chinese villain Lin Foo has a strange and indistinguishable accent, with the rolled "r's" of Spanish--he sounds anything but Chinese. I would place the time of this episode before the movie serial, which came out in 1937, rather than after it. If it was later than that, it certainly would have been short-lived, because of the overall poor quality of the show.

LET'S PRETEND

This much-beloved program began on CBS in 1930 as *The Adventures of Helen and Mary*. It featured two children, Helen and Mary, who wandered through a fairy-tale land, and evolved into *Let's Pretend* sometime in the late 1930's. There is disagreement about the date among historians--Terrace (1981) said it was 1934; while Dunning (1976) places the title change in 1939. The scripts adapted well-known children's stories and fairy tales into pure radio adventure, and won award after award. The driving force behind the show was a former actress named Nila Mack, who was described by *Newsweek* as "large, plump, hard-boiled and amazingly shrewd" ("Mack and the beanstalk," p. 108). She joined the show soon after its beginning as director, and wrote the adaptations based on stories by Hans Christian Andersen, the Brothers Grimm, Andréw Lang and others, as well as writing some original scripts. Nila Mack thought that children should be playing many of the roles, and she had as many as 50 child actors at a time working on the show, many of whom graduated to Hollywood. Others stayed with the show and later played adult roles. Nila Mack died in January of 1953, and *Let's Pretend* went on without her until late 1954.

The show was sustaining until 1943, when Cream of Wheat began sponsoring it. It was produced in front of a studio audience of kids, and the host was "Uncle Bill" Adams. The openings featured some means of travel to the land of *Let's Pretend*--a train, plane, roller coaster-- accompanied by the appropriate sound effects.

The program of August 10, 1946, opened with the theme music, followed by the children singing the Cream of Wheat jingle: "Cream of Wheat is so good to eat--Yes, we have it every day. We sing this song--it will make us strong, and it makes us shout 'Hooray!' It's good for growing babies, and grown-ups too to eat. For all the family's breakfast you can't beat Cream of Wheat!" Next, Uncle Bill: "Cream of Wheat--the great American family cereal--presents *Let's Pretend!*" The studio audience cheers loudly. He continues: "That's the way to say 'Hello' and 'How are you'--well, thank you, audience. And now, how about that story?" The audience shouts, "What are we waiting for?" Uncle Bill replies, "What are you waiting for? Well, Gwen, that's your department--what's today's story?" "Oh, it's one of the all-time favorites, Uncle Bill--'Faithful John.'" Uncle Bill says, "Oh, that's one I know. And how do we travel to *Let's Pretend*?" Gwen says, "Today that's in Arthur Anderson's department." Arthur tells us, "I'm all for a ride on the roller coaster--to get cooled off." Gwen says, "Well, Arthur, that's fair enough. All set, everybody?" Voices reply, and she counts: "A one, a two, a threeeee!" (Sound effects: roller coaster) Uncle Bill says, "It's time for *Let's Pretend,* and 'Faithful John!' Don't stand up in the seat and hold on to your hats!" We hear the roller coaster and screams of delight. "Oh boy, this is what I call fun, Uncle Bill! Start kinda slow, and then all of a sudden you get going like a sky rocket, flying along with the wind." Uncle Bill replies, "Yeah, almost like eating Cream of Wheat for breakfast, isn't it, Gwen?" Of course this leads into a commercial. The theme music comes up, and then: "Once upon a time, in a country beyond the sea, the beloved old King passed to his reward. Then it was that his son Richard was proclaimed the new ruler. As our story opens, we find the young King is being shown through the ancient corridors of the old castle under the guidance of his father's devoted and faithful servant, John." They come to a room that is locked at the old King's request, but Richard insists that John open it. Inside is a statue of a beautiful girl--the Princess of the Golden Heart, who loves anything made of gold. Richard falls in love with her, in spite of John's warnings. The young King has all the wealth in the kingdom converted to objects of gold, and they sail across the sea and lure the Princess on board with jewelry of gold. While she is distracted, they leave the harbor, kidnapping her. The King declares his love for her, and they sail for home. When they reach home, we hear the sound of crows flying over them--the crows are talking, and John overhears them tell that the Princess is surrounded by a spell--the King's horse will bolt and the King will be killed, and the Princess will fall into a deep sleep and die, unless someone pierces her shoulder and draws three drops of blood. This will break the spell, but that person will turn to stone. Of course all this comes to pass, and Faithful John kills the King's horse, brings the Princess out of her spell and is turned to stone, in order to keep his promise to the old King. The young King is filled with remorse, and several years later finds a sorcerer who says he can restore John's speech. He does, and John tells them that he can be alive again only if the King will take his sword and cut

off the head of his little son. He prepares to do so over
the objections of the Princess, because he has given his
word. But as he raises his sword, John comes to life and
tells him that his willingness to sacrifice what he loves
most was enough to break the spell. The theme music
comes up, and the audience cheers. After a commercial
for Cream of Wheat, the *Pretenders* for the day come in
and tell which roles they played. "Music conducted by
Maurice Brown. *Let's Pretend* is dramatized and
directed by Nila Mack. Would you like to see a broadcast
of *Let's Pretend*? Well, if you live in or near New York,
just drop a postcard to Cream of Wheat, CBS, New York
for your free ticket. And next Saturday, be sure to join us
when Cream of Wheat will take you on another magic trip
to the land of *Let's Pretend* to celebrate our sixteenth
birthday with the story of 'The Elves and the Shoemaker.'
(Theme music comes up) This is Bill Adams saying
remember to eat Cream of Wheat, the great American
family cereal. This is CBS, the Columbia Broadcasting
System." The theme music comes up and the audience
cheers.

　　　The show won awards and may have been
applauded by parents everywhere for presenting
children's favorite stories, but its appeal to kids was really
not so much different than the thrillers. After all, fairy
tales were full of witches and sorcerers and spells and
other scary stuff, not to mention plenty of violence or the
threat of violence (such as the possibility of a man cutting
off the head of his young son). Nila Mack was a master at
writing radio drama, and the sound effects and dialogue
were excellent, as was the acting of her young troupe of
Pretenders. The show had the earliest air date of any of
the shows described, and lasted almost as long as any of
the other children's programs.

LITTLE ORPHAN ANNIE

The first of the Children's Hour serials brought the little curly-haired girl with the round eyes right off the comic pages to the Blue Network on April 6, 1931. The show was produced for Ovaltine by the Blackett, Sample and Hummert advertising agency of soap opera fame (Barnouw, 1968), and capitalized on the cliffhanger format developed in the movie serials. This led the way for the rest of the juvenile serials--the climax of one story line (usually occurring on a Friday) and the beginning of a new plot to keep the listeners hooked.

The early shows were set mostly in Tompkins Corners where Annie lived with Mr. and Mrs. Silo, and featured the adventures of Annie and her pal, Joe Corntassel (played part of the time by Mel Tormé) and her dog Sandy ("Arf!"). Sandy was played by an actor aptly named Brad Barker. The other characters from Harold Gray's comic strip also appeared: Oliver "Daddy" Warbucks, the giant Punjab and the sinister Asp. If Annie was in trouble, one of them was sure to appear to rescue her. Later Annie's adventures, like so many of the other Children's Hour shows, expanded to much more exotic places.

The show was popular with the younger set; after all, the heroine was supposed to be nine or ten years old and did all kinds of things real kids that age could never do, such as rescuing folks who were at the mercy of crime lords or spies. However, parents were not as fond of Annie and her cohorts. A 1933 *Scribner's Magazine* article described Annie's adventures:

Annie, the leading character, is an orphan,

and the escapades which comprise the child's day-by-day life approximate a high degree of sadism. She has been kidnapped, chloroformed, rendered unconscious by a deliberate blow on the head, held prisoner several times, pursued over the countryside by the law, imprisoned in barns and hovels and freight cars. She has trailed and captured bank thieves. She has been forced to spend several nights in a deserted shack in the woods to avoid being taken back to a sadistic orphan asylum which is under the direction of a shrew. She has been taken back to the orphan asylum through a procedure obviously unjust, if not illegal, and there has been made to scrub floors and perform the labors of a sub-menial (Mann, 1933, p. 314).

When the show started in 1931, the network connections were not complete, so there were two casts performing the same script each day; one in Chicago and one in San Francisco. When the lines were completed, the Chicago cast was heard on all the stations (Stedman, 1971, p. 181). The show went to Mutual in 1937, then back to NBC, and finally to Mutual in 1941. Ovaltine and *Little Orphan Annie* were almost synonymous until Ovaltine dropped the show in 1940 to sponsor *Captain Midnight.* Quaker Puffed Wheat picked up sponsorship and a new character was introduced, Captain Sparks. He bore an amazing resemblance to *Captain Midnight,* and poor Annie's role was reduced to that of sidekick to Sparks. The show lost ground, and left the air in 1943. Premium offers added to the show's popularity; *Little Orphan Annie* masks, rings, badges signifying that kids were members of Radio Orphan Annie's Secret Society. These could be had simply by sending a seal from a jar of Ovaltine.

The earliest shows began with a song: "Who's that little chatterbox, the one with pretty auburn locks? Who can it be? *Little Orphan Annie!* Always wears a sunny smile, now wouldn't it be worth your while if you could be like *Little Orphan Annie?* ('Arf!' says Sandy.)" But sometime during the thirties, the lyrics were dropped, leaving just the melody played on an organ.

The episode of March 1, 1940, began with sound effects of an airplane, followed by a train whistle, then two toots on a ship's horn. The theme music came in, fading under announcer Pierre André's words: "Why do you suppose Aunt Lydia wanted Daddy Warbucks' workmen to disappear? Will Annie find out today? And say--have you found out how much better the new 1940 chocolate flavored Ovaltine is?" The commercial featured a letter from a listener, and ended, "The most important thing about the new sweet chocolate flavored Ovaltine is how it can make you be as husky and full of pep as Annie herself. And now, our adventure with Annie!" The narration continued, explaining how the workmen had been kidnapped from Daddy Warbucks' dam at Tombstone Hollow. The men had been rescued, and Jed Harbold, one of the kidnappers, had been captured. But the question is, why were they kidnapped? Annie, Joe, Daddy Warbucks and John Gage confront another kidnapper, old Pap Spears. (The Children's Hour was full of old Western characters with Walter Brennan voices.) Pap confesses he was hired to do it by Aunt Lydia Harmon and reveals that Jed Harbold is actually John Harmon, her son, who had joined a circus years before. But why didn't Aunt Lydia want the dam to be completed? Seems that Daddy Warbucks had brought in young Doc Walton because the area had no doctor. This "riled" Aunt Lydia, who had been doing the healin' in these parts. But where did the bear come from? Pap informs us the "b'ar" was brought by John Harmon to scare the men away. The "b'ar" was part of his circus act, and was "an awful old b'ar, and really pretty tame." They all start up the mountain trail to Aunt Lydia's, when they meet her coming down the mountain. They confront her with Pap's confession--Aunt Lydia is angry. "Ya ol' lizard!" Pap tells her, "Keep away from me--ya got me in enough trouble already, ya ol' witch!" Daddy Warbucks informs her that they will take her to the law in the nearest town, one of the few times the villain in a *Little Orphan Annie* story is given the opportunity to face the law. (Usually they were dispensed with by Punjab or the Asp.) Aunt Lydia begins musing about the view--Haunted Plateau on the other side, with a river gorge between. Suddenly she runs straight for the edge of the gorge. John pursues her, but too late! She jumps! The others are astounded. Joe tells us, "Gosh, one big leap right out into the air and 200 feet straight down to the river." A shaken Pap says, "I ain't never seed anything like that before." Suddenly we hear the sound of a plane approaching--it's a big plane! Where can it land around here? Looks like it's heading for Haunted Plateau! Daddy Warbucks thinks he knows who the pilot is. Pierre André provides the wrap up designed to keep the youngsters in suspense. "Say--what is the meaning of that airplane making a landing at Tombstone Hollow? And so soon after that dramatic leap over the cliff by Aunt Lydia Harmon. Seems to us that Aunt Lydia's wild way of getting out of going to jail was enough excitement for quite a time to come--but that airplane probably means that there's a brand new kind of excitement in store for us. Yes, sir, it looks as if March is going to be a big important month for Annie and all her friends. And remember, if you're a real friend of Annie's, you've got something important to do tonight before dinner. Fix yourself a mug full of the new sweet chocolate flavored Ovaltine to have with dinner--and that's the way you show how much you like Annie's adventures and want them to keep coming to you on the radio! Well, with Aunt Lydia gone and Jed Harbold and Pap Spears captured, it looks as if the trouble our friends have been having at Tombstone Hollow is at an end. But what about that big airplane that appeared so suddenly? I suspect it means the start of some wonderful new adventure for Annie. We'll find out Monday, so be sure to be here and until then, this is Pierre André saying goodbye."

The plots of the *Little Orphan Annie* shows were fairly intense. This particular one was the only one of the Children's Hour programs described here to do away with the villain by means of suicide, a subject forbidden on children's shows even then. Whether Aunt Lydia escaped death somehow is not known; regardless, the resolution was severe for a show aimed at young children. But *Little Orphan Annie* is probably not remembered so much for crime and gore, as for one of radio's most famous and perfect premiums--the "Little Orphan Annie Shake-up Mug." Kids had to get mom to buy Ovaltine so they could get the inner seal to send for the mug, which they could then use to mix up more Ovaltine. The mug had pictures of Annie and Sandy on it, with Annie saying, "Leapin' Lizards! For a swell summer drink, there's nothing like a cold Ovaltine shake-up mug, eh, Sandy?" (Stedman, 1971, p. 196).

THE LONE RANGER

One of the best-known characters, the Western hero whose radio career spanned over 22 years and helped start a network, was the Masked Man of the Plains, *The Lone*

Ranger. The show was first heard January 30, 1933, in Detroit over WXYZ. The station had been purchased by theater chain owners George W. Trendle and John H. Kunsky (who later changed his last name to King). WXYZ was a Columbia outlet, but Trendle didn't like the network's programming policies and dropped CBS in June, 1932. As an independent, WXYZ began losing $4000 a week (Bryan, 1939, p. 21). Trendle needed programming, and he decided that WXYZ could produce its own drama. One of the first projects was to be a children's show, with an Old West theme, and Trendle visualized his Western hero as a modern Robin Hood. A free-lance script writer named Fran Striker was hired, and was paid four dollars a script. The Lone Ranger of Striker's first scripts was a happy-go-lucky fellow, reminiscent of Douglas Fairbanks' Zorro; but Trendle didn't see him that way. He wanted a dignified, educated-sounding man, so the Lone Ranger became stern, and all traces of humor disappeared. Reports on how the silver bullets and silver horseshoes came about differ--some say the idea came from a Robin Hood script Striker had written, others say it was another Western script in which the hero used silver-tipped arrows. In either case, the silver bullets gave the great white horse his name. "The William Tell Overture" was chosen to be the theme music, after a search for music that would go with a gallop. This and all the classical music used by WXYZ was in the public domain, which was more economical.

In radio it was always necessary for the hero to have someone to talk to, so by the tenth script the faithful Indian companion Tonto had appeared. That story told how the Lone Ranger got his name--a group of six Texas rangers were after the infamous Butch Cavendish gang. Unfortunately, they were ambushed, and five (including Captain Dan Reid, the Lone Ranger's brother) were killed.

The Indian Tonto happened upon the scene; buried the dead Rangers and made an additional grave, so the gang would not know there was a survivor. He nursed the man back to health, after telling Reid that the other Rangers were dead. "You Lone Ranger now." Striker had selected the Indian's name from a map, without knowing that a "tonto" was an Indian who behaved badly (Osgood, 1981). Tonto was, for virtually the entire series, a former Shakespearian actor named John Todd. He was the only one of the cast who knew anything firsthand about the Old West, having traveled there with a Klaw and Erlanger Road Show (Bryan, 1939, p. 138). When Todd began the role, he was in his sixties, and he was past eighty when he acted in the last live *Lone Ranger* broadcast. Trendle fired him once because of his age, but the complaints from the listeners forced him to reconsider (Osgood, 1981). Todd occasionally fell asleep between scenes requiring his appearance--the most well known incident was the time he and the Lone Ranger were supposed to be on the second floor of a hotel. When the Lone Ranger said, "Let's go, Tonto," Todd had lost his place in the script and jumped ahead to "Git 'em up, Scout."

The popularity of the Masked Man and his faithful Indian companion grew by leaps and bounds. In May, the Lone Ranger offered a free Lone Ranger gun to children who wrote in for one. Two days later, the guns were gone; in another two days, the Lone Ranger was on the air, begging the kids to stop writing. The station received over 24,000 letters. In July, the Detroit Department of Recreation held its annual School Field Day on Belle Isle, and it was announced that the Lone Ranger would be there. A crowd of 20,000 was all Belle Isle would hold, so when 70,000 children showed up, the Lone Ranger himself had to restore order (Bryan, 1939, p. 131).

The program was sold to Silvercup Bread, with the first commercial broadcast in November. By the middle of 1934, *The Lone Ranger* was also heard in Chicago over WGN and in Newark over WOR. These stations, along with WXYZ and WLW in Cincinnati, were the nucleus of the Mutual Broadcasting System. WXYZ joined NBC Blue in September of 1935, but continued to feed *The Lone Ranger* to Mutual. The program was first offered by transcription in 1938--it was heard on 140 stations by 1939, and on 249 stations by 1953, with estimated audiences of 12,000,000 listeners each week (Osgood, 1981, p. 283). Not all were children, however. *The Nation* reported the results of a 1941 survey showing that at least 63 percent of the audience were adults (Boutell, 1941, p. 44).

The first actor to play the Lone Ranger is generally believed to be Jack Deeds, followed by George Stenius, but Dick Osgood (1981) of the WXYZ staff reported it was just the reverse. (Stenius later changed his name to Seaton and became a Hollywood producer.) But by April, 1933, Earle Graser had taken over the role. Graser had never been west of Michigan and had never ridden a horse, but his voice had just the right dignified resonance that Trendle wanted. Graser was the Lone Ranger until April of 1941, when he was killed in an automobile accident. Surely no child of the era who was a regular listener could ever forget that voice--or how strange it was when the voice changed. It was necessary to have the Lone Ranger wounded and written out of the show, with Tonto left to carry on for a time by himself. When the Lone Ranger returned, the voice was somehow different. The new Lone Ranger was Brace Beemer, who had announced the show, and he remained in the part until the end of the broadcast. Beemer looked the part of the Ranger more than had Graser--he was tall and was a horseman. Other characters on the program

were played regularly by John Hodiak and Frank Russell;
some by Danny Thomas.

The success of *The Lone Ranger* could be
attributed to several things: first, Trendle's surefire formula
which was never tampered with; second, the "do's" and
"don'ts"--he must use good English, and he must always be
on the side of law and order, no smoking, swearing,
drinking, shooting to kill, no love affairs, no slang, and
never do any wrong whatsoever. The "better-radio-
programs-for-children" group had few complaints about
The Lone Ranger, and the show was applauded by the
General Federation of Women's Clubs, the Parent-Teacher
Associations--even J. Edgar Hoover, who was quoted in
Time as saying that *The Lone Ranger* "is one of the
greatest forces for juvenile good in the country" ("The
masked rider," 1952, p. 78). Even though the shows met
the approval of parents, they were still full of violence. A
study of the violence content of the children's radio
thrillers showed *The Lone Ranger* episode in the sample
to contain the most incidents of violence, although there
were no killings. Of course all the episodes were complete
stories, 30 minutes long, so if violence was there at all, it
would be part of the script; whereas some of the serialized
programs might have the violent content clustered in one or
two episodes (Boemer, 1984).

The character made the transition from radio to the
movie serials in 1938, and to cartoon strips. Striker was
writing 60,000 words a week with all these endeavors (plus
writing *The Green Hornet* and *Sergeant Preston of the
Yukon*), and his salary grew to $10,000 a year. *Time*
reported that the radio show and the character were
grossing $5 million a year by 1952, with most of the profit
going to George Trendle ("The masked rider," 1952, p.
78). When television arrived, the Masked Man and Tonto

moved to the small screen, but without Beemer and Todd. The last live radio broadcast was September 3, 1954. Recorded broadcasts were heard until May 27, 1955 (Osgood, 1981, p. 323).

The program broadcast June 12, 1942, began with the familiar strains of "The William Tell Overture," and the sound of hoofbeats coming in with the music. Then the famous voice crying, "Hi Yo, Silver!" and the sound of gunshots, then the announcer's voice, "A fiery horse with the speed of light, a cloud of dust, and a hearty Hi Yo, Silver! *The Looone Ranger!*" The music comes up, then under, "Listen now, radio neighbors, to a thrilling adventure of the Masked Rider of the Western Plains, as the bakers of fresh, vitamin enriched Merita Bread and delicious Merita Cake bring you another exciting transcribed story of *The Lone Ranger,* Champion of Justice and Right!" The commercial for Merita followed, then the stirring music returns. "With his faithful Indian companion, Tonto, the daring and resourceful Masked Rider of the Plains led the fight for law and order in the early Western United States. Nowhere in the pages of history can one find a greater champion of justice. Return with us now to those thrilling days of yesteryear. From out of the past come the thundering hoofbeats of the great horse Silver--*The Lone Ranger* rides again!" Music comes up, and the voice of the Lone Ranger: "Come on Silver--let's go, big fellow! Hi Yo, Silver, awaaaaaayyyy!" The announcer sets the scene: "It was early evening when gunplay broke out at the K-C Ranch. (Sound effects: crowd yelling) Betty Turner and her young sister Janie owned the ranch, and times had been hard. There'd been but a few cowhands when the rustlers came. They did their best to overtake the thieves, but their best was not good enough." Nate and Sam, the usual faithful ranchhands, tell

Miss Betty it was the Hood Milford gang, and they offer their savings to the sisters to help them. Miss Janie returns from town and tells her sister about an Indian who asked her a lot of questions about their ranch. The Lone Ranger and Tonto ride up, and after convincing the sisters they are not part of the gang and telling them he knew their late father (the Lone Ranger knew someone everywhere he went), the Ranger tells them he has devised a plot to trap Milford. He wants them to keep some cattle for a while, and they will be paid for doing this. Meanwhile, Hood Milford and his henchman meet a man at the saloon. It turns out he is Captain Miguel Lopez, head of a band of Mexican revolutionaries. Milford's gang is stealing cattle and selling them to the Mexicans for food. The Lone Ranger and Tonto are watching them, but suddenly they are confronted by Nate and Sam, who take them at gunpoint to a woods to find out what's going on. The Ranger takes away their guns with the help of Silver, and tells them of the plans. The cattle arrive, and Nate and Sam realize who the cattle were stolen from (they were stolen from the Army), and they drive the cattle away from the Ranch. The Lone Ranger tells Nate and Sam that the Cattlemen's Association has offered a reward for the capture of the rustlers, and he wants the girls to have the money. He shows the two men a silver bullet, and they finally realize who he is. He tells them that the group of revolutionaries will be baited with the cattle. Later, at the saloon, Nate and Sam tell Milford the rustlers have been captured, all but their leader. The Army had arrived just in time to arrest the revolutionaries and the rustlers, but the Lone Ranger had arranged it so that Lopez escaped to confront Milford in the saloon full of people. They are all arrested, the K-C Ranch gets their cattle back, plus the reward put up by the Cattlemen's Association for the capture of the rustlers. The

Lone Ranger, who never takes a reward for himself, has seen to it that the sisters got the money. The ending to the episode followed a fairly standard formula: the Lone Ranger takes leave of the folks he has rescued; they are talking about him, and how the problem was resolved. Miss Janie says, "Gosh, I'd sure like to see that man without his mask!" But there is never a hint of romance for the Masked Rider of the Plains. Then the voice of the Lone Ranger comes from off mike, "Hi Yo, Silver, awaaaayyyy!" Theme music in, followed by another Merita commercial. The announcer concludes with, "The story you have just heard is a copyrighted feature of *The Lone Ranger, Incorporated.* (Music up to close) More exciting adventures await you, radio friends, when the Lone Ranger rides again in defense of justice and right!"

The episode of May 9, 1945, was sponsored by Cheerioats (former name of Cheerios) and the opening had the addition of the cereal's name, whispered in rhythm with galloping hoofbeats. In this episode, the Lone Ranger and Tonto see a wanted poster signed by Sheriff Weaver which describes them and offers a $5000 reward! Two men have been impersonating them, and robbing people. The Ranger and Tonto rescue a woman from the pair, who escape. They escort her back to town, where they are chased by a posse led by the Sheriff, finally to a box canyon. There the Lone Ranger disguises himself as a cowhand, and helps capture Tonto. He and one other man are strangers, but the Sheriff has both men try to ride Silver, to determine who owns the great white stallion. Of course Silver is instructed to throw the Lone Ranger, and allow the other man to ride him. The man is arrested (he is the real outlaw), and his cohorts plot to break him out of jail and rob the mine office. They bring Tonto along so that he and the other man will be captured. But the Lone Ranger captures them;

he sees to it that the young couple gets the reward, and he rides away.

Of all the programs of the Children's Hour, *The Lone Ranger* scripts were among the best. Striker wrote stories that were fast-paced and filled with action. The plots were involved enough to be interesting, but at the same time, logical enough to be believable. The actors' voices always let the listeners know whether the character was a "good guy" or a "bad guy," making the story line easier to follow. The endings were "happy" because the criminals always got what was coming to them and the victims got back whatever they had lost. Premium offers included badges and guns, and *The Lone Ranger* Safety Club had well over a million members. The young members pledged not to cross streets except at regular crossings, and to look both ways; and to not play in the streets and always tell the truth (Boutell, 1941, p. 45). It's not difficult to understand why *The Lone Ranger* outlasted most of the Children's Hour programs. There was also a *Lone Ranger* book, *The Lone Ranger Rides,* in 1941, and the television program, which began in 1949 and lasted until 1965, with re-runs lasting much later in some markets.

MARK TRAIL

Man of the wilderness, early environmentalist, comic strip hero--*Mark Trail* came to radio in early 1950. The show was based on the long-running Ed Dodd comic strip, and featured Mark and his friends Scotty and Cherry, and the big dog Andy. Together they battled the bad guys who would ruin their first love--the wilderness, where the stories took place. This was probably the first program to bring to the kids the message of protecting the wilderness and the creatures who lived there.

The *Mark Trail* episode dated December 1, 1950, began with the announcer's voice shouting, "Kellogggg's Pepppp! (music sting follows) Kellogg's Pep, the build-up wheat cereal with a prize in every package, invites you to share another thrilling adventure with (echo) *Marrrrk Traaaaail!* (Sound effects: storm) Battling the raging elements! (Sound effects: howling wolves) Fighting the savage wilderness! (Sound effects: hoofbeats) Striking at the enemies of man and nature--one man's name resounds from snow-capped mountains down across the sun-baked plains--(echo) *Marrrrrk Traaaail!* (music sting) Guardian of the forests--(sting) protector of wildlife--(sting) champion of man and nature--(sting) *Marrrrrk Traaaaail!* (theme music up and out) The plush and paneling of W. Putnam Clyde's office suggests serenity and soft speech. But there is no serenity and soft speech in the office now. In front of Mr. Clyde's desk stands Dan Brady, his eyes furious with anger. Equally as angry is Mr. Clyde as he listens impatiently to the other." Brady has come to tell Clyde to stop dumping poison into the lake, because it will ruin the lake, the businesses and the town. Clyde says he doesn't care what happens to them--he'll continue to operate, even if "it means wiping out every living thing in the country." After a commercial for Kellogg's Pep, we join Mark and Scotty as they are ready to go fishing in Pine Tree Lake. When they get to their boat, they discover a bad smell and lots of oil on the shoreline. When they get to the middle of the lake, the situation is worse--more oil and dead fish. They head for Pine Tree Falls to see fishing guide Dan Brady, who tells them about Clyde's factory up the river and how he's been dumping old oil in the river. Mark goes to see Clyde, and invites him to go fishing; then tells him about how he is upsetting the balance of nature by polluting the lake. Mark suggests ways he could stop the pollution, but Clyde tells him it would cost money, and shows him the door. Scotty bursts in and tells them that Dan has been thrown in jail for trying to smash the pipe that lets the oil into the lake. Clyde accuses Mark of trying to distract him while Dan is smashing the pipe, and threatens him with jail also. After the commercial, we join Mark and Scotty visiting Dan in jail. Mark has an idea, and enlists the help of Doc Stevens, a friend of Clyde's. Doc takes Clyde to the middle of the lake to meet a "prospective customer." It's Mark, of course, who tries to interest Clyde in fishing. Clyde angrily demands to be returned to his factory, so Mark rows him up the river. But when Clyde lights a cigar and tosses the match overboard, the oil on the river begans to burn! Mark rows furiously and they get out of the fire. The fire burns through the drain pipe and sets the factory afire. Clyde attacks Mark, and the oars fall over the side. Clyde (in an abrupt change of character) becomes contrite as the boat drifts toward Pine Tree Falls, and Mark tells him they'll have to swim for it. Clyde admits he can't swim, and urges Mark to save himself. But Mark casts his fishing line to the shore and hooks a tree, and the boat swings into shore. They walk back to the factory, which has been saved by the townspeople of Pine Tree Falls. Clyde admits he was wrong, and will clean up lake and restock it with fish--on the condition Mark takes him out and teaches him to fish! After a music sting and the sound of hoofbeats, the announcer returns: "Listen! That's Satan, a wild horse that is the terror of the Wyoming prairie. Six men have died trying to trap this devil horse--will Mark be the seventh victim of the devil's herd? Tune in again, same time, same station, on Friday, and find out what happens to--*Marrrrrkk Traaaaaail!*" The opening is repeated.

   Mark Trail is perhaps typical of the programs of the late forties and early fifties, when some of the

Children's Hour programs began to develop a social conscience. The script was one of the more educational of those reviewed, with its emphasis on explaining the balance of nature, and how companies could avoid pollution of rivers and lakes. Also typical of the later shows, the action depended on dialogue and sound effects rather than narration, and the voices were easily distinguished. This was one of the 30-minute episodes, which were broadcast from early 1950 until sometime in 1951 on Mutual three times a week. From 1951 to 1952 the show went to ABC, where it became a 15-minute five-day-a-week serial.

NO SCHOOL TODAY
(BIG JON AND SPARKIE)

One of the storytelling and variety shows designed for the younger children, *No School Today* was the creation of Jon Arthur. The show with that title ran on Saturdays on ABC for two hours at first, and later 90 minutes. *Big Jon and Sparkie* was the shorter weekday version, 30 minutes the first year, then 15 minutes in 1951. The shows were mostly composed of stories and songs, and came on the air in 1950. Arthur did most of the characters, including the voice of Sparkie, an elf, who had a "Chipmunk" type voice, created by a speeded-up playback of the previously taped dialogue.

An undated 45-minute portion of one of the Saturday morning programs began with the theme music, "Teddy Bears' Picnic." Next is the voice of Sparkie:" "Hey, Big Jon, I see by the paper here that a scientist has just crossed a potato with a sponge." Big Jon replies, "Hey, that sounds great. How does it taste?" "Terrible--but it sure holds gravy." Big Jon laughs--"Seems like I heard that joke once before on our program." Sparkie asks, "What

program's that?" "*No School Today*--with Big Jon and
Sparkie." Sparkie says, "Oh, yeah--I'm Sparkie." "And that
makes me Big Jon, I guess." The theme music comes up.
Then they talk about the show for the day, which begins
with a song by television puppeteer Shari Lewis and her
two puppet characters, Lamp Chop and Charlie Horse.
After the song, Sparkie tells Big Jon about chapter 311 of
his current favorite "movietime serial," a story of space
adventures with Captain Jupiter, interspersed with vocal
sound effects by Sparkie. After the story, it's "March
Time" with Gilhooley Mahoney and his internationally
famous Leprechaun Marching Band. (An instrumental
march is played.) Big Jon returns with, "Now, our
storyteller--*The Singing Lady,* Ireene Wicker." She tells the
story of "The Magic Fishbone," by Charles Dickens. After
this fairly lengthy segment, Shari Lewis, Lamb Chop and
Charlie Horse sing another song. Big Jon and Sparkie
return with time for "inspection" with the Magic Spyglass.
Big Jon mentions that they don't have much time, "because
of our long feature story, about Washington Irving's
Legend of Sleepy Hollow, so I'm just going to look into the
Spyglass here, and Sparkie, I'll nod to you and you mark
down the score and we'll figure it out and see who wins
today, the boys or the girls." He's checking for cleanliness
first, hands, face, well-groomed, including clean, combed
hair and being well-dressed in clean, neat clothes--shoes
clean and shined. He takes a quick look at their rooms, and
they go over the scores, which the girls win--again! Then
follows the story classic, *Legend of Sleepy Hollow,* told
mostly by a narrator with music background, with a few
lines by other voices. Big Jon then asks Sparkie to preview
the next week's show, but he tells Big Jon it's a secret.

The program, which consisted of Big Jon and
Sparkie's showcasing of other personalities and a children's

classic (all presumably from recordings) was well produced and loved by the younger set of listeners. Certainly there was nothing objectionable about the content, which stressed good habits along with the stories and songs. The sound of Sparkie's voice was no doubt a real novelty then, although by today's standards somewhat difficult to understand. The show was one of the last children's radio shows, running until the late 1950's (Dunning, 1976).

POPEYE THE SAILOR

Popeye and his gang, girlfriend Olive Oyl, J. Wellington Wimpy, adopted son Matey, enemy Bluto and the others were never quite the success on radio that they were in the comics, and certainly never achieved the popularity of the cartoons that were so loved by children both in the movies and on television. The musical effects on the programs were supplied by Victor Irwin's Cartoonland Band, giving it the distinctive sound associated with the early cartoons. The show came on NBC in 1935, and moved to CBS for a short run in 1936.

A *Popeye* episode (not dated) began with the familiar song--"I'm Popeye the Sailor man, I'm Popeye the Sailor man, I yam what I yam 'cause I yam what I yam, I'm Popeye the Sailor man." (Beep-beep) Then the announcer: "Wheatena's his diet, he asks you to try it, with Popeye the Sailor man." Then there's a commercial for Wheatena with the cartoon-sounding music and a little girl's voice. Then the announcer sets the scene: "Now since Matey's been going to school, he's started reading about storybook characters that are all new to him. One day he's fighting imaginary Indians, the next he's off with King Arthur to his court or out hunting dragons and giants. Matey, Wimpy and Popeye have had supper at Olive's, and, as it's getting

late, Popeye thinks it's about time to start home." Matey
says he wants to see giants, so Wimpy takes Olive's potted
geranium, gives it some of Popeye's favorite cereal
(obviously Wheatena) to transform it into a giant geranium.
They climb the geranium, and there is the giant's
castle--with a sign on the door saying "Anyone by the name
of Jack keep out--this means you!" Matey says he wants to
see a giant, so they knock on the door, which is answered
by a lady giant. She invites them in, because none of them
are named Jack--Jack would give the giant indigestion!
Olive begs her not to cook them and serve them to the
giant. The giant's wife hides them, but of course the giant
returns home and discovers them. Popeye doesn't get to
eat his favorite cereal, but Matey tricks the giant into letting
him eat some (he'll make a better meal after eating it).
Matey subdues the giant, and they make their escape down
the geranium, which shrinks back to its original size.
Wimpy says, "If it was only a dream, it was a pleasant one,
for we all shared the same excitement." Popeye replies,
"Them's elegant thinkin', Wimpy, and anyways, all the
giants in this here world is make-believe, and if you all
knows it, oh, you can have a lotta fun poppin' 'em." After
another commercial, Popeye sings again, "I yam what I
yam 'cause I yam what I yam, I'm Popeye the Sailor man."

With the musical effects (done by Victor Irwin's
Cartoonland Band) used in place of sound effects, and the
voices being so similar to those used on the cartoons, the
show sounded much like a cartoon sound track. Whether
or not this was detrimental to the show's popularity is not
known. The story was obviously aimed at very young
children with the clever adaptation of the old favorite fairy
tale, *Jack and the Beanstalk.* The voice characterizations
and the effects made the program actually superior to most
of the other children's shows broadcast in the early thirties.

RED RYDER

"America's famous fighting cowboy," red-haired *Red Ryder,* was first seen in a 1938 comic strip created by an ex-cowboy, Fred Harman. The N.E.A. syndicated strip had, according to *Time,* a following of thirteen million readers. This made him a natural for radio, and *Red Ryder* came to the Blue Network in 1942. However, soon after, NBC Blue was successful in getting *The Lone Ranger* away from Mutual, and dropped the fledgling serial. Mutual grabbed it up and broadcast *Red Ryder* against *The Lone Ranger. Time* reported that the first Hooper ratings gave the edge to *Red Ryder* in this radio shoot-out between the two cowboy heroes ("Hi-yo, Silver," 1942, p. 65).

Red lived in Painted Valley with his aunt "Duchess" and his young Indian ward, Little Beaver. MacDonald (1979) noted that this was one of the first racially mixed radio families, reflecting the effort to combat bigotry that came into vogue on the Children's Hour during the 1940's (p. 205). Little Beaver usually had a part in solving whatever problem Red took on, which gave the listeners another child hero to identify with.

A 1948 episode began with the announcer: "From out of the West comes America's famous fighting cowboy, *Red Ryder!* Say--what in the world is happening at Painted Valley Ranch, with Red trying to lay off half the hands, and the punchers breaking into open rebellion! Well, it'll all come out in the story, 'Pint-sized Pinto,' and believe you me, it's a yarn you won't want to miss one word of. Now, just before we turn back the covers on tonight's grand story of the West that lives forever---" Then the theme music, "The Dying Cowboy," comes in. "A lot of the fun and

excitement in the old West was in the breeding and
exhibition of fine horses. You know, in these stories of the
West that lives forever, we've all heard a lot about Red's
coal black stallion, Thunder. But his little Indian sidekick
has a pinto horse of which every one in Painted Valley is
plenty proud. As tonight's story opens, we find ourselves
at Painted Valley Ranch. Buckskin, Little Beaver, the
Duchess, and Red Ryder all seem to be quite excited." They
are discussing the horse show, which they expect the pinto,
Papoose, to win. Buckskin wants to bet on the pinto, but
Red admonishes him--"Bettin's one thing we don't do
around here." Duchess begs off from going into town with
them, as she doesn't feel well. They want to call the
doctor, but she won't hear of it. In the next scene, they are
at the rodeo and horse show, and Papoose wins the pinto
class as expected. Red and Buckskin congratulate Little
Beaver, and the man whose horse won second place, Alec
Carter, comes over and offers to buy Papoose for $3000--"a
heap of money." They turn him down and head for home,
where they see the doctor just leaving the ranch. They ride
to catch up with him, and he tells them that the Duchess is
ill, and must take it easy. Red says, "The trouble is, she
forgets she's a woman and keeps thinkin' she's an iron
man." The doctor says it's her heart, and she must have
three months of nothing but rest and sunshine, in a place
like Hot Springs, but it's expensive--a thousand dollars a
month. Red is worried--winter is coming and money is
tight this time of year. Besides, the Duchess flatly refuses
to consider it. The doctor tells Red he should convince her
to go--if not, "I'm afraid you'll be wearing a mourning
band before you bring your cattle up to the summer range."
Red, Buckskin and Little Beaver gather in her bedroom,
and she becomes upset and is gasping for breath. Red
insists that he'll sell off the herd now, even though he

won't get much for them and send her to Hot Springs. Little Beaver interrupts, and is told, "Little Beaver--you know the old sayin' don't you? Children are to speak only when they're spoken to." Red goes to the bunkhouse to tell the hands he'll have to lay off half of them, even though he told them they'd have jobs for life. Old Amos says, "You're not layin' me off." He suggests that they all take a 50 percent cut in pay until the Duchess is well. Red refuses, but the men insist. They began to round up the cattle, but they are scrawny and Red doesn't think they'll bring enough money. Little Beaver keeps trying to tell Red he wants to help, but Red brushes him off, so Little Beaver rides for town. Buckskin tells Red he thinks the child has gone to sell his pinto, so they ride after him. After a commercial for Langendorf Bread, we find Little Beaver riding for Alec Carter's ranch, where he agrees to sell Papoose. Carter writes a check, and they go outside. Little Beaver begins to cry, and Red and Buckskin ride up and stop the deal, telling Carter why Little Beaver decided to sell the pony. Carter rides over to the ranch with them, and loans them the money to send the Duchess to Hot Springs. Little Beaver asks why she's crying--"Crying? Why, you onery little redskin, can't you see when a person's happy? And you all can tell that pill-roller I don't need his foul-tastin' tonic--I found the finest medicine any woman ever had--the love of her friends and her family." The theme music comes up and under the announcer: "Listen again this Thursday, and every Tuesday, Thursday and Saturday nights at 7:30 for the adventures of *Red Ryder.* "

This particular episode had no violence, no crime, no thrilling adventure. It did, however, have some of the realities of life as it probably was in the old West--illness and not enough money. It had plenty of old-fashioned ethics--hard work, family love and neighborly love, and willingness to sacrifice. The pioneer spirit dictated "you take care of your own." Children, although loved, had their place--"speak only when spoken to." This might have made *Red Ryder* a bit tame for the kids who wanted crime and hard-riding adventure, but nonetheless, the show lasted into the 1950's, and was on television in a 30-minute syndicated show in 1956.

RENFREW OF THE MOUNTED

The first of the Westerns to use the "Mountie" theme was *Renfrew of the Mounted,* which started on CBS in 1936 as a 15-minute serial, three times weekly. However, the show moved to the Blue Network the next year, and adapted the 30-minute format (Dunning, 1976). The hero was Inspector Douglas Renfrew of the Royal Canadian Mounted Police; and every kid knew that the Mounties *always* got their man.

The episode of February 4, 1939, began with sound effects: the cold north wind howling, and the cry of a wolf (twice). *"Rennnnfrew! Rennnnfrew of the Mounnnnnted!"* (Sound effects: police whistle) "Renfrew reporting. Ready for action!" The announcer says, "Once again, we bring you *Renfrew of the Mounted,* another story of the famous Inspector of the Royal Canadian Mounted Police, known to thousands of admirers through the books and stories of Laurie York Erskine, adapted for radio by George Ludlum. Today, Renfrew investigates the strange case of Corporal Malcolm Sandes, officer in charge of the Police Post at Glenafton, who has been suspected of taking a bribe. Our story begins in Glenafton itself, frontier town of British Columbia, where officials of the local bank are looking forward to a busy day. Outside, a light rain spatters the windows, and a group of mounted strangers are quietly

gathering at the bank's door. But inside, everything is light
and warmth. Unaware of danger, the president is in his
private office, talking with an assistant." The bank
president shows Jackson, the assistant, a newspaper article
about a nearby bank being held up by the Saltire Gang.
They discuss the possibility of its happening to their bank,
and the president asks how they could protect themselves.
"Well, sir, the men at the windows have revolvers, of
course." The president suggests they should think about
such things as tear gas and extra guns, but Jackson believes
they are well protected because of the Mounted Police Post
in their town. The bank president agrees that this really is
the best protection any bank could have. The cashier
comes in and reports to the banker they have close to
$40,000 in cash on hand; suddenly there is a commotion
outside--it's a holdup by the Saltire Gang! Shots ring out,
and the gang gets the money. The bank president calls the
Mounted Police Post, but it is closed; then he calls
Renfrew! Renfrew orders all the roads covered to Fort
Brandon. Renfrew and the others can't figure out why
Corporal Sandes wasn't on duty, when he was ordered to
stay because of the holdups. They meet Sandes just outside
of town. He confesses that he was given a $1000 bribe by
Saltire. But why would Sandes accept a bribe? Renfrew
says he doesn't believe it, and the Corporal says that's all
that matters to him. Sandes goes on to explain that he got a
call the day of the holdup, saying Saltire had been seen near
Coalville Ranch, so he rides there, only to discover it was a
plant. On his way back, he met an old Indian on the trail,
who gave him the money and a note. The Indian had been
given the money two days earlier with instructions to give
it to Sandes, but delayed because he was tempted to keep
the $1000. "So there it is. Saltire thinks I'm a bribed
man." One of the other Mounties rides up to them and gives

Renfrew a message from the Constable at Fort Brandon--Saltire's gang has been seen riding toward Black Pass Canyon! Sandes rides away to find Saltire, to throw the bribe in his face! Renfrew sends one of his men to head off Saltire at Black Pass Canyon, but then orders him to let Saltire through! Renfrew plans to dynamite the pass, so Saltire will be trapped in the Canyon, with only one way out. The Mounties hide in the cabin at the pass. Renfrew is worried about Sandes, who is young and headstrong. After Saltire rides through, they plan to follow and dynamite the pass. Suddenly shots ring out! They ride after the gang, who shoots at them! Renfrew believes the only reason they were fired on is that they have already shot a Mountie--Sandes! Renfrew and the others look for Sandes. They find blood on the trail, then the young Corporal, shot through the heart. He had his hand on the money, ready to throw it in Saltire's face. Renfrew and the others capture the gang, shooting the gun out of Saltire's hand. One of the Mounties, Foster, wants to hang Saltire on the spot, and Renfrew says he'll hang, all right, but not there. "Foster--telephone down to Maryvale--tell them that Corporal Sandes' job is finished." (Sound effects: wind howling) *"Rennnnnfrew! Rennnnnfrew of the Mounted!"* (Sound effects: wolf howls, twice) "So we bring to a close another adventure of *Renfrew of the Mounted,* famous Inspector of the Royal Canadian Mounted Police, known to thousands of young Americans and Canadians through the books and stories of Laurie York Erskine, and especially adapted for radio by George Ludlum. The case included House Jameson as Renfrew, Bradley Barker, Joseph Curtin, Harold Debecker, Monty Meacham, Brent Sargent, Carl Eastman, Robert Dryden, Grant Gordon, and Soomer Alberg. Next week at the same time, the story, the 'Cat Robe Treasure Cape.' *Renfrew of the Mounted* is a program of the National Broadcasting Company."

Renfrew of the Mounted had enough action and shooting to hold the listeners' interest, with a bank robbery, blood on the trail, dynamite and a murdered Mountie. The voices were fairly distinctive, and the sound effects were typical of the late 1930's, in that they sounded a bit contrived. The show was also typical of the Western set in contemporary times--there were telephones, but apparently no cars. In the West, everyone had to travel by horseback. The show lasted off and on into the 1940's, and was on television in 1953.

RIN TIN TIN

The only one of the Children's Hour programs with a non-human hero in the title roll was *Rin Tin Tin*. The show was one of the earliest of the thrillers, and started as *Rin Tin Tin Thrillers* on NBC Blue in 1930. The 15-minute early version, which lasted until 1934, starred the German Shepherd movie wonder dog, who performed all manner of heroic feats (Dunning, 1976). Program premium offers included samples of dog biscuits, an identification locket for a dog's collar, a book of dog biographies and pictures of Rin Tin Tin himself (autographed?) (Eisenberg, 1936). The adventures of the great dog and his young master, Rusty, returned to the air, this time on Mutual as a 30-minute show in 1955; thus making the show one of the earliest as well as one of the latest programs. It ran on ABC-TV from 1954 through 1961, then moved to CBS television where it was on until 1964.

The episode broadcast November 13, 1955 (from the second run) began with the sound of reveille. "The National Biscuit Company presents the adventures of *Rin*

Tin Tin!" We hear Rusty, "Yo, Rinty!" (Sound effects: dog
barking) A singing commercial comes in under the barking,
sung in military cadence: "Rin Tin Tin, Rin Tin Tin, Rinty,
Rinty, Rin Tin Tin, Rin Tin Tin is brought to you by
Shredded Wheat and Milk Bone too. Rinty and Rusty, side
by side, loyal, heroic, the Regiment's pride. Action, drama,
you'll find them in--the thrilling adventures of *Rin Tin
Tin!*" The instrumental music comes up and under the
announcer. "The National Biscuit Company presents this
week's adventure of *Rin Tin Tin,* entitled 'Rin Tin Tin and
the White Buffalo.'" After a commercial for Nabisco
Shredded Wheat done by Rusty and the announcer, we
hear: "Lieutenant Rick Masters speaking, officer of the
101st Cavalry, stationed at Fort Apache. We're known as
the fighting Blue Devils. To keep peace in the territory we
patroled, it was necessary for us to sign treaties with the
Indians. These treaties were respected and honored by both
the White Man and the Indian. To help the Indian, we'd
been given the detail of surveying the territory, and setting
up certain boundary markers so that the Indian would know
what land was theirs and to show the White Man what part
of the territory belonged to him. We were at work on this
surveying and marking job when we became involved in a
very unusual affair. It all began one morning when we
were hard at work: the patrol, myself, Rusty and Rinty." A
group of Indians ride up to them, and Rick explains why
they are there--to protect the Indians' hunting grounds from
the White Man. The Indian, Komali, says, "This is good.
When the sun leaves the sky, you will come to the camp of
Sakarow, my father, to feast and smoke the pipe of peace."
Rick replies, "It is agreed. May your father live a hundred
years." Komali replies, "May you be present at his funeral."
Rusty begs to go with the Indians to their camp, and he and
Rinty are permitted to do so. They see a herd of buffalo,

and the Indian tells Rusty that the White Man is destroying the herds, and thereby destroying the Red Man by taking away his source of food and hides. The Indian rides down the hill to kill a buffalo, telling Rusty to stay there because the buffalo is dangerous, especially when wounded. Komali kills the buffalo, and Rusty starts down the hill, but suddenly two white men appear with guns, to take the buffalo away from the Indians! Rusty sends Rinty for Lieutenant Masters. Some of the men leave to drive the buffalo to their land, but the Indian jumps the one that remains! In the scuffle, Rusty gets the gun--the man thanks him, but soon finds out Rusty is on the side of the Indians! Rusty holds the men until Rick arrives. The man, Garth, wants the Indian arrested for attacking him, but Rusty says he saw the whole thing. Garth wants to know whose side the Lieutenant is on--Rick says, "Whichever side is right." Garth says he's right because he is white. Rick replies, "Right or wrong isn't settled by the color of a man's skin, Mr. Garth." The other braves return, having captured the rest of the gang, and Komali agrees to let them go, with Rick's promise they will not return to the Indian's land. After a commercial for Milk Bones, "Rick Masters again. Garth and Keller and the other two men rode away, but there was hate and vengeance in Garth's every action and in his eyes. I had a feeling that we hadn't heard the last of them, but I was hopeful. That night, all of us made our way to the camp of the Cherakawas. We all gathered around the huge council fire. Once we were settled, the peace pipe was passed to me by Sakarow, the chief of the Cherakawas." Meanwhile, Garth and his men are spying on them. Garth says Apaches killed his parents, and he wants revenge. At the council fire, the chief talks about Rusty's courage, and says, "May his eyes behold the White Buffalo." Rick tells Rusty that it's a famous legend.

Suddenly shots ring out, and the chief is killed! Rick and
the men ride to find Garth, ordering Rusty to stay there.
The chief's son, Komali, rides with them to find his father's
killer. The next morning, Rusty is talking to Rinty and the
dog starts barking excitedly--he has found Garth's trail!
They follow it and find the men. Rusty holds the gun on
Garth and sends Rinty for Rick. Garth turns and runs,
knowing Rusty won't shoot him in the back--but he runs
directly into the path of a buffalo stampede! Rusty is also in
the path of the herd, but suddenly the White Buffalo
appears and the stampede parts to let Rusty escape! Garth is
killed; later Rusty tells Rick and the Indians what he saw,
and the Indians believe him. "The legend says you'll find
him if your heart is brave and true; and you treat all men as
brothers, no matter what they do." Rinty barks in
agreement. After a Milk Bone commercial with the
announcer, Rusty and Rinty, we hear Rick say, "As soon as
Komali was out of sight, we mounted our horses and
headed back to Fort Apache. We didn't talk, we just
remained quiet with our thoughts. And the words of the
song seemed to come back--If your heart is brave and true.
Yes, we are all brothers. You know, almost every man has
some particularly trying time in his life. And one of our
troopers went through such a stage: Corporal Boone. It all
began when Boone decided to leave the service and get
married. The whole business became quite involved and
exciting." Rick and Sergeant O'Hara talk with Rusty about
Boone's getting married, serving as the preview for next
week's story. "Don't forget, next Sunday at this same time
over this station, another exciting chapter in the adventures
of *Rin Tin Tin,* presented by the National Biscuit
Company, makers of Milk Bone Dog Biscuits and Nabisco,
the original Shredded Wheat. For the adventures of *Rin
Tin Tin* on television, consult your local paper for time and

station. Don Morrow speaking, this program came to you transcribed from New York." The military theme music comes up.

This example of the later run had everything needed for a successful children's show--action, sound effects, the old West, buffalo, Indians, the Cavalry; and a hint of the supernatural--the White Buffalo. The voices were quite distinctive--Rusty sounded very young, and Rinty barked and growled his way through the script. The scripting (especially the Indian's dialogue) was clever and imaginative; and was designed to combat bigotry, a popular theme in the later years of children's radio. The late addition of the show to radio with a simultaneous run on television ensured a short run. Had it returned to the air at an earlier date, *Rin Tin Tin* surely would have enjoyed a much longer run. A tape from the early run was not located.

THE ROY ROGERS SHOW

The King of the Cowboys' career was quite similar to that of radio's other singing cowboy, Gene Autry, with Rogers getting his start on radio, working as a ranch hand, and becoming a star of Western movies. Autry preceded Rogers with a regular radio show by four years, but both lasted on the air until the middle 1950's. Roy was first heard on Mutual in 1944, with a 30-minute show that was similar in format to *Gene Autry's Melody Ranch,* with songs by Roy and the Sons of the Pioneers, and a story about one of Roy's adventures. The show went to NBC in 1946, and wound up there in 1955 after returning to Mutual for three years in 1948. The program eventually put much more emphasis on the thriller drama, with primary appeal to the juvenile section of the audience. Along with Roy was his regular gang, composed of Dale Evans (Queen of the West), and Gabby Hayes (the counterpart of Autry's Pat Buttram), who was later replaced by Pat Brady. The Sons of the Pioneers were later replaced by other singing groups, including the Riders of the Purple Sage and the Mellow Men.

An undated episode (probably from the early 1950's) began with the announcer: "The *Roy Rogers Radio Show!* (theme music up) Yes, folks, it's the *Roy Rogers Radio Show* for the whole family! Adventure--suspense--mystery--and music; starring Roy Rogers, the King of the Cowboys, and Dale Evans, Queen of the West, with Pat Brady, the Mellow Men and an all-star cast. And now, here to greet you with a song and a story, are Roy and Dale." Roy and Dale sing a few bars of "Mexicali Rose," then Roy says, "Well, good evening folks, greetings again to the whole family. That song, 'Mexicali Rose,' reminds me of a trip that Dale and Pat and I made a while back. We'd been looking around for a real isolated guest ranch where we could take it easy for a few days, and the Rancho El Dobe looked just right. It's down in the desert country, about 20 miles this side of the Mexican border, and the town of Mexicali. Before we got there, Dale made me promise that I'd do nothin' but rest and relax. And when we checked in, Mr. Wilson, the owner of the Rancho, guaranteed that we'd have a nice, quiet vacation. Well, the next morning, we got up early and decided to give the horses a little exercise before breakfast." While riding in the desert, Roy and Dale and Pat discover the body of a man--who has frozen to death! Roy deduces the body must have been dumped there, and Dale reminds him they're supposed to be on vacation. "Let the sheriff handle it." They return to the Rancho to call the sheriff, and Pat tells Mr. Wilson about it while they are ordering breakfast.

Wilson offers them fresh cantaloupe. Later, Bradley, special investigator with the Border Patrol, comes to speak to Roy and tells him the man was Lopez, one of their best men, who was on the trail of a smuggling gang. He asks Roy to help, by going to the other side of the border and buying souvenirs, including diamonds. Bradley cautions Roy not to tell anyone, not even Dale. They go to Mexicali to go shopping, and Roy asks the girl who has taken their pictures where he can buy diamonds. A man comes up to introduce himself as Popescue, and offers to sell Roy family heirlooms--diamonds! Roy goes with him to see the diamonds, which are offered for $10,000, but Roy says the duty on them will double the price. Popescue says he will arrange to have the stones delivered across the border, duty free! He will take Roy to the man who will deliver the diamonds. Meanwhile, Dale and Pat are worried about Roy, and they ask the girl who took their picture about Popescue. After threatening her with calling the police, she agrees to take them to Popescue. In the meantime, Roy and Popescue have gone to see the smuggler, who realizes Roy is a spy and hits him over the head. They plan to freeze Roy and dump his body on the other side of the border! They take Roy to the train station, and put him in a refrigerator car. But the smuggler tricks Popescue into getting into the car and shuts him inside with Roy! The train leaves, and Popescue tells Roy he is sorry. Suddenly the train stops, and they hear a dog barking. It's Bullet, Roy's dog, and Dale and Pat rescue them! They bundle up like Eskimos, and get back in the car, where they trap Mr. Wilson, who is the head of the smuggling ring. The tip-off was his serving them cantaloupe for breakfast--the only place he could have gotten it that hour of the morning was from a refrigerated railroad car! Dale tells Roy they're going home to the good old Double Bar R, where they can get rested up from their vacation. Roy concludes the story, "And folks, that's the story I'm always reminded of whenever I hear the song, 'Mexicali Rose.'" They sing the song, including a verse in Spanish. "That's all for now, folks. This is Roy Rogers, sayin' to all of you from all of us, goodbye, good luck, and may the good Lord take a likin' to ya. See ya next week!" The announcer finishes with, "You've been listening to the *Roy Rogers Show,* starring Roy Rogers, King of the Cowboys, and Dale Evans, Queen of the West, with Pat Brady, the Mellow Men and an all-star cast. Be sure to be with us next week at the same time."

This appeared to be one of the later shows of the series, with very little emphasis on singing. Dunning (1976) placed the episodes of this type in the 1950's, and it did have many similarities in production and style to the other radio shows of that period. There were an abundance of sound effects, an intricate plot, and relaxed, natural-sounding dialogue, including the humor provided by Pat's massacre of the English language. The plot became a bit far-fetched with the frozen body. Apparently it didn't matter to the young listeners that, if a body were frozen, the cantaloupe would be frozen also. Roy and Dale continued after the demise of the radio show with movies, and a television show that ran from 1951 to 1957.

SERGEANT PRESTON OF THE YUKON (CHALLENGE OF THE YUKON)

If *The Green Hornet* was *The Lone Ranger* set on the streets of a big city, then *Sergeant Preston* was *The Lone Ranger* transposed to the Canadian Northwest. All three scripts were written by Fran Striker and produced by George W. Trendle's crew in Detroit, and the plot formulas were much the same. The "Mounties," or Royal Canadian Mounted Police, had always held a fascination for American kids, and the show was one of the more popular and long running of the Children's Hour. The original *Challenge of the Yukon* started out in 1939 as a regional 15-minute show in the Detroit area, and Dick Osgood (1981) of the WXYZ staff recalled that the original story was created by Tom Dougall, whose father had lived in the Canadian Pacific (p. 147). Classical music was used for the theme, like the themes for the *Hornet* and the *Ranger*, and with Preston was the wonder dog, Yukon King, the "swiftest and strongest lead dog in the Northwest." The show went to ABC as a 30-minute program in 1947, then to Mutual in 1950 where it stayed until leaving the radio in June of 1955, and running on television from 1955 through 1958. The title changed sometime in the 1950's to *Sergeant Preston of the Yukon.*

A 1947 episode began: *"The Challenge of the Yukon!"* This was followed by the sounds of the dog barking over howling winds. "It's King, swiftest and strongest lead dog of the North Country, blazing the trail for Sergeant Preston of the Northwest Mounted Police in his relentless pursuit of lawbreakers." More barking, and Preston's voice, crying, "On, King! On, huskies!" The announcer continues over the sound of the wind, "Gold--gold discovered in the Yukon! A stampede to the Klondike in the greedy race for riches! Now, back to the days of the Gold Rush, when Sergeant Preston and his wonder dog King battle through storm and snow to preserve law and order as they met--*The Challenge of the Yukon!* (Sound effects: wind howling) In a small cabin hidden in the mountains about a half-mile from the trail that led south from Dalton City, three men sat around the pot-bellied stove. Buck Nelson dominated the other two. The look of cunning on his face contrasted with the weak and small stature of Pete Remus, one of his companions, and the stupid look of the other, Mike Able. Buck sneered as he listened to the whining voice of Pete." Pete believes they have enough money and should quit. The rumor is that Sergeant Preston is on their trail, but Buck wants to get even with Preston. The lookout, Dick, comes in the door and tells them someone is coming up the trail. They shoot the man, and drag him to the cabin to search him for money. All they find is a letter addressed to "Father John Murphy." "Bah! No wonder he ain't carryin' any money--he's a priest!" They break open the box he was carrying on his dog sled, and find it full of gold. Pete is worried; he thinks it's bad luck to kill a priest. Buck decides to throw Pete out so they can split the money three ways instead of four. Pete begs to stay, but Buck makes him leave. Later, Sergeant Preston finds Pete, snow blind and wandering waist deep in the snow. Preston sends Pete to Jim Taylor's roadhouse, a couple of miles down the trail, with King to guide him there. Preston says he'll pick King up on his way back from Indian Village. Pete lies to Taylor and says he's supposed to take King with him to Dawson City; then he takes King to the cabin. He is counting on Buck to take him back. Buck says he'll shoot the dog, and someday he'll get Preston. King is looking frantically for an escape from the cabin--he jumps out a window with Buck shooting at him. King is hit! He rolls over and over down a steep hill, and crawls into a cave, leaving a trail of blood! Preston returns to the roadhouse, finds that King is gone and goes to look for him. In the meantime, a wolf has found King--he attacks, but King kills the wolf. Preston has been looking for King, and Pat knocks on his door to tell him that they are worried about Father Murphy, who is coming up to the new mission. Suddenly, they hear King barking, and see that he's been shot. The next morning, Pat and two other men go with Preston to backtrack where King has been. They find the dead wolf, and climb the steep slope that King rolled down. They see the cabin, and split up to surround it. No one is there, and Pat comes to tell him that they have captured two men who were watching the trail. Buck and Pete return, and Buck tries to escape--he falls and hits his head on the corner of the box that belonged to Father Murphy. He is dead! Certainly poetic justice prevails. The theme music comes in, and the announcer concludes, "*The Challenge of the Yukon* is a copyrighted feature originated by George W. Trendle and brought to you each week at this time. All names and incidents used are fictitious. Listen again next week for another exciting adventure during the days of the Gold Rush. The part of Sergeant Preston was played by Paul Sutton. Fred Foy speaking--this program came to you from Detroit."

The episode had everything that the young listeners could want--adventure, violence, murder, an amazing dog, plenty of sound effects and a little twist to the plot ending to add excitement. The format is typical of the later shows, with dialogue and sound effects setting the scene, and plenty of action. The only time the narrator must carry the story is when the dog is on his own--King might have been an amazing dog, but he couldn't talk! Naturally, right prevails and the criminal gets what's coming to him. The later shows were sponsored by Quaker Puffed Wheat and Quaker Puffed Rice, the cereal shot from guns, so gunshots and the cereal were tied in nicely together in the opening. *Sergeant Preston of the Yukon* was one of the last two children's thriller dramas on the air (the other was *Bobby Benson*.) The last live broadcast was June 9, 1955, and transcribed re-runs were on for another year (Osgood, 1981, p. 329).

THE SINGING LADY

One of the very earliest children's radio storytellers, *The Singing Lady* came to NBC Blue in January of 1932. She was Ireene Wicker, who was certainly a "one-woman band." She wrote and produced the 15-minute program of stories, and was its sole talent. She told stories designed for the really young listeners, interspersed with songs that were part of the stories. All the narration was done in her natural voice, and she used other voices to play all the parts necessary to tell the stories. Dunning (1976) said that she added the extra "e" to her first name when a numerologist told her it would bring her great fortune (p. 526). At any rate, she was certainly successful as *The Singing Lady,* lasting on radio until the early 1950's. Mothers especially liked the show for its lack of violence and "blood and thunder."

An undated episode opens with Ireene Wicker humming the theme and playing the piano. "*Jack and the Beanstalk*--an old English fairy tale." She then sings the intro to the story about Jack, and does the voices of Jack and his mother, also the wife of the giant and the giant himself! She embellishes the story somewhat by having Jack's father held captive by the giant and rescued by Jack. Then, she tells the story of *The Red Shoes,* in which a little girl named Karen wishes for a pair of magic red shoes that will make her dance like a ballerina. The shoemaker, who is a magician, tells her the price for magic shoes is "tears, heartache and loneliness." She puts on the shoes and becomes a grown-up ballerina who can't stop dancing. She winds up in the carnival, dancing with tears, heartache and loneliness. She has to wear out the red shoes by doing good deeds. Once again, Ireene Wicker does all the voices of the characters while a piano plays in the background.

The Singing Lady was obviously quite talented--her range of voices was extensive and added greatly to the stories. The very young listeners were most likely attentive to her stories, but it's doubtful the show was much competition for the thrillers among the older children.

SKIPPY

The exploits of the comic strip character created by Percy Crosby came to radio as one of the very first children's adventure programs, shortly after *Little Orphan Annie* made her way to the airwaves in 1931. There was also a movie which starred Jackie Coogan about the character (Terrace, 1981). The radio show ran first on NBC, and went to CBS in 1932. It lasted until around 1935. Unfortunately, very little is known about this important early bit of juvenile radio, and no recording of the show was located. *Skippy* was mentioned by several writers: Eisenberg's (1936) book on the listening habits of New York children gave brief program descriptions. This is what he wrote:

Skippy. This program was taken from the famous cartoon by the same name. The content, however, is altogether different. Skippy usually has his two friends, Sooky and Carole, with him. His adventures are rather unusual for a modern city boy. He always gets out of trouble with ease and agility. He plays the character of a good and, all-too-often, misunderstood boy. --WABC, Mon. through Fri., 5:00-5:15 P.M. (p. 213).

Eisenberg also listed the program's premium offers: membership in a secret society, code badge and secret directions for a handshake.

The *Skippy* of Crosby's comic strip had a checked hat, a tie and a big white collar. He was a self-confident kid, with humor and philosophy mixed together (Churchhill, 1967, p. 247). Eisenberg's observation that the content of the radio show *Skippy* was entirely different from the comic strip *Skippy* was probably correct, for the show was one that was invariably mentioned in the articles condemning the children's thrillers. Arthur Mann (1933) wrote in *Scribner's Magazine,* about an episode of *Skippy:*

> The program is sponsored by the Washburn-Crosby Company for the purpose of selling Wheaties, a dry cereal said to be of pressed whole wheat. Tuning in, I find Skippy and his father captives in a truck and being taken to a hideaway. They have been kidnapped to prevent their testifying against "The Brain," a super-criminal. Some time ago, "The Brain" was at the head of a counterfeit ring, which Skippy broke up. At the time I tuned in the super-criminal is suspected of pyromania, for several buildings in the town have been burned. These episodes have been going on for months. The announcer assures each anxious juvenile listener that, while he or she may be gasping with suspense and at the point of swooning, there should be no deep concern over the ultimate preservation of Skippy's life. He will come out unscathed (p. 313).

SKY KING

Sky King was successful as a radio show, but is perhaps better known as an early television program, running from 1951 through 1954, with these episodes re-run through 1966. The adventures of the ex-FBI agent, ex-Navy pilot and rancher as he fought evil in the American West and other locales was first heard on ABC in 1946 as a 15-minute daily serial. By 1947 the show had become a 30-minute, complete story format sponsored by Peter Pan Peanut Butter. It went to Mutual in 1950 and lasted until 1954. Sky zoomed around in his plane, the *Songbird,* with his young niece Penny and his nephew Clipper, and combined two of the young listeners' favorite types of heroes--pilots and cowboys.

One of the later episodes from the early 1950's began with the voice of "Peter Pan" and a short commercial, then the announcer: "Peter Pan Peanut Butter presents---(Sound effects: plane diving)--*Sky King!*" The plane sound segues into the theme music. "Today--'The Mark of El Diablo!' (Music up) Winging south, the *Songbird* is over border country, over the desert where the first cattle trails from Mexico crossed, bringing into old Arizona the beginnings of its cattle industry. Now the land is silent--sun stricken, forgotten. But in the *Songbird,* Sky King is gazing down at a small red flicker in the distance. As it grows into tongues of fire leaping into the desert, Penny, Clipper and Jim stare down with unbelieving eyes." They see that it's a ranch house, burning to the ground, and they go down to get a closer look. Penny sees a masked rider, dressed all in black on a black stallion, but Clipper thinks it was her imagination. They land and find a piece of paper addressed to Link Higgins with a warning written

on it, and signed by "El Diablo." Sky tells them that El
Diablo was the name of a spread where there was a bitter
feud 50 years before. Todd Odell was the man involved,
and he vowed to come back and finish the job. Naturally,
Odell *always* dressed in black. They go to another ranch
to warn the owner, and they hear gunfire. They find the
man, Dan Kemper, unconscious with the same warning
clutched in his hand, and a hoofprint on his forehead! It
must have been made by the black stallion ridden by El
Diablo! After a Peter Pan commercial, we join a meeting of
the owners of the small ranches, who have all received the
same warning. They are all scared, because they think it's
the ghost of Todd Odell. Sky and Clipper ride in search of
the stallion, and when they find him, Sky drops down onto
his back. Because there was something strange about the
hoofprint, and this stallion has been shod, Sky knows it
wasn't the horse that made the print. Suddenly, one of the
ranchers, Zack Morley, is on a ridge above them, firing at
them! Penny flies over in the *Songbird* and lays down a
smoke screen so they can escape. Sky and Clipper capture
Morley and his partner and tell them they're taking them to
jail--a jail without bars or jailers! Sky and Clipper fly them
out to a forsaken spot by a waterhole and leave them, with
a hidden walkie-talkie behind a rock. The men talk about
Apex Rubber Company--a company which probably wants
the land because of a plant that grows there that can be
made into rubber. Meanwhile, Penny and Jim are captured
by El Diablo at the burned-out ranch house--he has a club
with a horseshoe nailed on the end! After a Peter Pan
commercial, El Diablo tells them he's informed the
ranchers that Sky King is helping him, and he wants to
know where they have taken Morley. Meanwhile, Sky and
Clipper are riding for the Higgins place with the ranchers in
pursuit. Sky hits El Diablo, and his mask falls off,

revealing that he is really Link Higgins! It turns out Kemper is the grandson of Todd Odell and is inheriting the land. The announcer concludes the story: "Once again, *Sky King* wins out in his constant fight for justice. All of the grocers of America who sell Peter Pan Peanut Butter make this program possible. Peter Pan outsells all others--it's America's favorite. Right, Peter Pan?" Peter Pan replies, "Right, Mike. Tell your mom to look for me in my bright green dress on the Peter Pan jar." The announcer concludes, "*Sky King* features Earl Nightingale, Beryl Vaughn, Jack Bivens. Mike Wallace speaking. Listen Thursday to *Sky King*--(Sound effects: plane)--and the Vanishing Arabians!" The theme music comes up.

This was another program typical of the 1950's, with sophisticated plot and dialogue, plenty of sound effects and lots of action. But the Code of the West is still present, and right prevails, with the bad guys brought to justice. An indication of loosening restraints on the role of women was the important part Penny played in helping--after all, she flew the plane and helped Sky and Clipper escape; a refreshing change from the "helpless female" roles in so many of the earlier programs.

SMILIN' ED'S BUSTER BROWN GANG

Smilin' Ed McConnell was a long-time radio singer and storyteller, who joined the *Buster Brown Gang* in 1944 on NBC. The program became a sort of variety show for kids, with stories told by Smilin' Ed and dramatized with the regular cast of actors, plus music and sound effects which were the highlight of the show. The live studio audience of children laughed and cheered for his regular cast of imaginary characters, which included Squeaky the Mouse, Midnight the Cat, Froggie the Gremlin, and

Grandie the Piano (who emphasized what Smilin' Ed said with musical notes).

The show from May 15, 1948, began with the squawk of a parrot--"Awk, there's plenty of loot, awk--plenty of loot." The voice of a pirate, laughing-- "There's plenty of loot, Captain, all right!" The announcer comes in with, "Kids, don't miss this exciting pirate story--and here to tell it is Smilin' Ed McConnell!" Music background comes up, and Smilin' Ed says, "Yes, kids, you better come a runnin', it's ol' Smilin' Ed and his Buster Brown Gang! (He sings) I got shoes, you got shoes--why, everybody's got to have shoes! And there's only one kind of shoes for me, good ol' Buster Brown Shoes!" He laughs, and the audience cheers wildly. "Oh yes, sir, Buster Brown is on the air, out here in Hollywood with Smilin' Ed and Squeaky the Mouse and Midnight the Cat, Grandie the Piano, and ol' Froggie the Gremlin, and we gonna start our program off right now with our story, so don't you miss it!" The theme music for a pirate story ("Yo, ho, blow the man down") comes up, then: "Well, here we go, kids, to the Spanish Main for another story of the desperate pirates who risked their lives for stolen gold several hundred years ago." The story begins with Smilin' Ed's narration--the story is set in the West Indies, where a boy named Juan Hernandez owns a beautiful green parrot named Poll, who talks and repeats everything she hears. Juan and his father are listening to the parrot talk, when suddenly there is gunfire! The town has been attacked by pirates! After a commercial for Buster Brown Shoes (punctuated by Grandie the Piano), Juan's father and mother talk about their losses--they are penniless--Juan bursts in to tell them that the parrot has also been stolen by the pirates! Next, we hear the pirates discussing their loot--which includes Poll. Later, the pirate ship returns to the island, but all the pirates are dead of yellow fever! Senor Hernandez tells his wife and son that the pirates always bury their loot on an uninhabited island, and he knows where they have been, because there is red clay on the sides of the ship, and there is only one island where the red clay may be found. Juan wants to go along to help his father. They sail to the island, where they see a house. There is no one at the house--except Juan's pet parrot! They search the house for a map, but the parrot talks, repeating what she has heard from the pirates and tells them where to look for the buried treasure. Suddenly the Pirate Captain appears, but the parrot distracts him and Senor Hernandez captures the pirate. Smilin' Ed says, "Oh, yes sir--I thought that was a pretty good story!" Froggie the Gremlin interrupts--"I'll sing the bubble-gum song, I will, I will!" Then we hear from Buster Brown and his dog Tige talking about shoes. Then Squeaky the Mouse plays his little bitty bells with Froggie and his accordion--"They gotta quit kickin' my dog around." Midnight the Cat says, "Niiice." Froggie the Gremlin still wants to sing his bubble-gum song, but Smilin' Ed says he has to become visible first--Froggie plunks his "magic twanger" and becomes visible--"I'm a gremlin, I am, I am." But here comes Alkali Pete the Cowboy, who is harassed by Froggie, who gets him all mixed up, to the delight of the young audience. Froggie sings his song about bubble gum. After another Buster Brown Shoes commercial, Smilin' Ed concludes: "And now, kids, don't you miss our program next Saturday mornin'. I'm gonna have a free gift for all of ya, so you be there at that radio--we have a wonderful story for ya 'bout Koola, and his magical genie of the jug, and Mr. Gymnasium, the athletic instructor, will be here too--and you know what happens when Froggie and Mr. Gymnasium get together. Oh, we're gonna have big doin's around here next Saturday, so don't miss it. And now--has everybody had fun around here today?" The children cheer wildly. "Oh, yes, we've got a big mob here today, and that's fine, buddies. Now don't forget church and Sunday school, and be listening next Saturday when you hear, 'Hi, kids! Come a'runnin'!' (He sings) The happy gang of Buster Brown now leaves the air, the happy gang of Buster Brown now leaves the air..." There is more loud cheering, and the announcer concludes: "The *Buster Brown Gang*, starring Smilin' Ed McConnell is produced in Hollywood by Frank Ferrin, and is directed by Hobart Donovan."

Smilin' Ed had a folksy, friendly way with the kids, and his ability to do the different voices of some of the characters such as Froggie made him a sort of an aural puppeteer. The harassing banter between Froggie and Alkali Pete was genuinely humorous, even to grown-ups. Smilin' Ed was on television in 1950-1951, and it seems likely that he helped set a pattern for a kids' variety show that was taken up on television by the puppets (Howdy Doody and Kukla, Fran and Ollie) and by Captain Kangaroo. The show lasted for eight years, nearly as long as any of the children's programs remained on radio.

SMILIN' JACK

The daredevil aviator created by Zack Mosley for the comics didn't achieve the radio popularity of some of the other heroes of the "funnies." Jack Martin, central character of the long-running strip and a movie serial, lasted only a short time on radio in a 15-minute serial on Mutual. Dunning (1976) says the show ran from February until May of 1939; however the episode obtained was dated December 18, 1939, and was supposed to be the first show of the series.

That show started with the music theme, then the announcer: *"Smilin' Jack,* now coming in on Runway Number One! (Sound effects: plane) Hello, everybody. Today and for the rest of this week, we're trying something entirely new on the air. We're presenting for your approval, a dramatic preview of a program we think you'll like. It's a public radio audition of the famous newspaper cartoon, *Smilin' Jack.* You've followed the romantic adventures of *Smilin' Jack* in your newspaper, you've seen him capture the hearts of beautiful girls like Dixie and Mary. And now, for the first time, you're going to hear him on the air. But remember, this is just a test. So if you'd like to have this program on the air regularly, you'll have to write and tell us so. But now, for---*Smilin' Jack.* (Music theme up) During the past few weeks, Jack has had little time to spend with his fiancée, Mary, having been drafted into the government's fight against an international spy ring, headed by a mysterious person known only as 'The Voice.' But now, because of a new development in the case, Jack has been ordered back to his own airport, and at this moment, accompanied by government agent J-4, is in his plane, streaking for home and Mary. J-4 is speaking." The agent asks Jack to take him down at Michigan City, because he's afraid there's a leak in the department--"The Voice" has ways of persuading people to talk, including kidnapping an agent's daughter. The young lady, Gail Sanderson, has been released and is to attempt to take them to the hideout of the spies. Gail is to meet Jack at the airport and pretend to take flying lessons from him. The line she is to use so that Jack will know her is, "Remember last night in St. Louis." J-4 tears up the memo with the code line and throws it out the window of the plane. Jack calls Mary and tells her he's on his way. Shortly after, a new mechanic named Riker comes to

Mary's trailer and spreads a rumor that Jack has been in St. Louis with another woman, and will be giving her flying lessons so they can spend more time together. Mary doesn't believe him, saying he must be talking about Downwind Jackson. Nonetheless, she promises to ask Jack about it without revealing how she found out. When they walk outside, Fat Stuff is waiting for her. Fat Stuff is "shadowing" Riker, and isn't in school--he's playing hooky, because he saw Riker snooping around Jack's plane the night before. We hear a sound of a button hitting the floor--he's popped another button off his shirt, and Mary asks him why he doesn't reduce. Jack lands, and Fat Stuff makes a hasty exit, because he knows he'll be in trouble with Jack for skipping school. Jack and Mary hug and kiss (more mushy stuff), and Jack tells her he has to give flying lessons--"Flying lessons? To a girl? A girl from St. Louis?" Mary says everyone is talking about it--but Jack denies it, and tells her he isn't allowed to say any more--he swears he wasn't in St. Louis, and that he has never seen the girl before. Mary believes him, but when Gail comes in, not only is she gorgeous, but she says, "What's the matter, Jack? Don't you--remember last night in St. Louis?" Mary runs away crying. The announcer returns with, "Oh, oh. Jack's certainly got himself in hot water this time! How's he going to square himself with Mary without violating his promise to J-4? And what about this mysterious adventure with beautiful Gail Sanderson? We'll hear more about it when we tune in on *Smilin' Jack* tomorrow. But remember this, as we told you before, this broadcast of *Smilin' Jack* is a public audition. You see, here's what we'd like to do--we want to try this program out on the air, let you listen to it and see if you like it. If you do, and if you'd like to hear it regularly, we think we could get a sponsor to put it on every day. But to convince him that you really like this famous cartoon character, and want to hear more *Smilin' Jack* adventures, we'd like for you to write and say so. And if you don't like Jack, write and tell us why not. Write today, won't you? Just address your letter to the station to which you're listening. Say what you think about Smilin' Jack and Fat Stuff and Mary--and be back with us tomorrow at this same time to hear what happens when the mechanic Riker, working for a band of foreign spies, sets out to wreck Smilin' Jack's plane." The plane sound effects come up, then the theme music.

Indications are that the show did run in 1939 for a brief time, so it seems likely that this initial episode may have been broadcast in December, 1938, rather than 1939. Like several of the other short-lived shows such as *Flash Gordon,* the emphasis on romance may have contributed to the program's downfall. After all, the aviator and spy theme would appeal primarily to young boys who were disinterested in such goings-on. Otherwise, the episode was marked by plenty of sound effects, easily distinguished voice characterizations and the possibility of plenty of action. This particular cliffhanger ending would have appealed perhaps more to the girls.

SPACE PATROL

The world of the 21st Century was the setting for the exploits of the members of the *Space Patrol*. The 30-minute adventure began on ABC in 1950, lasting until the demise of radio drama in 1955. The show was also on television from 1950 to 1956. The commander-in-chief of the *Space Patrol* was Buzz Corey, and the inevitable radio sidekick was Cadet Happy. Together they cruised space in the pursuit of interplanetary criminals.

An undated episode of the show began with the sounds of a rocket and "*Space Patrol!* (Rocket sounds up) High adventure in the wild, vast reaches of space! Missions of daring in the name of interplanetary justice! Travel into the future with Buzz Corey, commander-in-chief of the *Space Patrol!* (Sound effects: rocket) In today's transcribed *Space Patrol* adventure, Buzz and Happy are in the frozen polar region of Planet X. Pursuing Prince Baccharati into the shaft of an Enduria mine, they are unaware of a huge figure, lurking behind a shoulder of rock." We hear their footsteps and Buzz and Happy are talking softly--suddenly Happy is grabbed by the giant native! "I'll give him a blast with my ray-gun!" Music comes in, and the announcer returns: "And now, for the complete story of today's thrilling adventure of--*Spaaace Patrollll!* (Rocket sound up) And now, *Space Patrol's* adventure on the ice cap of Planet X! Commander Corey at last has Prince Baccharati in a position where the evil ruler of Planet X can be compelled to liberate hundreds of human beings whom he has forced into virtual slavery. With Buzz holding a ray-gun on the power-mad Prince, Baccharati has reluctantly ordered a fleet of his ships to come to the polar cap to transport the captive natives to their homes farther south. From the ship, the Commander is now supervising the evacuation by means of a short-range spaceophone, while Cadet Happy guards Baccharati and his assistant, Dr. Melengro." Corey speaks with Carson, the man in charge of loading the natives, who are mostly Thogs. Baccharati tells Buzz that the people may not allow the Space Patrols to land, but Buzz points out that most of them hate the Prince. Carson tells them that one of the Thogs has escaped into the mine--a Thog who is loyal to the Prince. Buzz tells him to let the Thog go, and he and Happy lock the Prince and Dr. Melengro into the aft compartment of the Prince's space ship. But the Doctor has an escape plan--he has discovered a metal cylinder in a secret compartment. It contains lirium 12, an irritant gas under pressure, which they can spray at Buzz and Happy to overpower them. Meanwhile, the Commander and the Cadet watch the last of the natives loaded into the mine train. The train leaves, and while they prepare for takeoff, they discuss the possibility that those who hate Baccharati might blow the ship away. Buzz goes to get Baccharati and Melengro, but the evil pair spray the gas at him and escape to the mine shaft, where they have hidden a space ship. There they encounter the escaped Thog. "Friends--you come safely." "Who are you?" "Me--Granu--overseer. Granu make all Thogs work hard." He asks to go along, and they tell him he must first kill the two men chasing them. Buzz and Happy enter the mine shaft, and Granu attacks them. The Prince orders him to kill the Space Patrolmen, but Granu refuses, so Baccharati shoots him with the ray-gun; Melengro turns the temperature control on the Space Patrolmen's thermal suits down to zero and leaves them all to die. The Prince and the Doctor return to the Prince's space ship outside, but discover that the spaceophone panel was smashed in the scuffle, so they are unable to call their men. They blast off anyway. Meanwhile, Buzz regains consciousness and turns up his heat control and Happy's. They go outside to look around and see that the space ship is gone. They go back into the mine and make friends with Granu, who wants them to take him in a "sky sled." He shows Buzz and Happy where the Prince had hidden the other ship (a small "atmosphere" ship), and they blast off. Meanwhile, Baccharati and Melengro approach the castle, but they are attacked and the ship crashes. They are uninjured, and a small atmosphere ship approaches. Of course it is the one

Buzz and Happy and Granu are in. They capture the Prince and the Doctor, and tell them their guard will be--none other than Granu! Music comes up, with rocket sounds, and the announcer returns. "Join us again next week for another thrilling adventure with--*Spaaaace Patrollll!*" The rocket sound effects come up, and the opening words are repeated.

Because the show ran unsponsored the first season and there were no commercials in this episode, it was probably from 1951. Typical of the later radio programs, there were plenty of good sound effects, and a really imaginative script, full of words created to describe people and technologies unknown. It was fast paced and action filled, with the "good" and "bad" voices the young listeners had grown to expect. Justice prevailed; and the villains got their just deserts, being turned over to the formerly loyal Thog they had left to die! This program dealing with the future and outer space had evolved considerably since the early days of *Buck Rogers* and *Flash Gordon*. *Space Patrol* was more similar in some ways to the early *Star Trek* episodes. Its popularity in the early 1950's is understandable.

STRAIGHT ARROW

Although Indians were plentiful in the Children's Hour programs of the old West, *Straight Arrow* stands alone as the only one with an "Indian" as the hero and title character. *Straight Arrow* was supposed to be a heroic Comanche brave who turned up mysteriously whenever there was danger. But the Indian was actually a young white rancher, Steve Adams, who had been *raised* as an Indian by the Comanches. He was sort of an old West Clark Kent, who rode to a cave on his ranch and

transformed himself into Straight Arrow. MacDonald
(1976) noted that the program presented the most
consistently positive image of Indians. The 30-minute
show started on Mutual in 1948, and lasted until 1951.

The episode of March 24, 1949, began with the
sound of Indian tom-tom drums, which became the
background for the commercial: "N-A-B-I-S-C-O, Nabisco
is the name to know, for a breakfast you can't beat, try
Nabisco Shredded Wheat!" (Done in a rhythmic monotone
to go with the drums) Indian music comes up and the
announcer says, "Keen eyes fixed on a flying target! (Music
sting) A gleaming arrow set against a rawhide string!
(Music sting) A strong bow bent almost to the breaking
point, and then-- (A note played on an organ simulates an
arrow flying through the air) *Straaaaight Arrow!* (Music
up) Nabisco Shredded Wheat presents *Straight Arrow,* a
new thrilling adventure story from the exciting days of the
old West. (Music up) To friends and neighbors alike, Steve
Adams appeared to be nothing more than the young owner
of the Broken Bow cattle spread. But when danger
threatened innocent people, and when evil-doers plotted
against justice, then Steve Adams, rancher, disappeared.
And in his place came a mysterious, stalwart Indian,
wearing the dress and warpaint of a Comanche, riding the
great golden palomino Fury! Galloping out of the darkness
to take up the cause of law and order throughout the West
comes the legendary figure of--*Straaaaight Arrow!* (Music
up) With the westward expansion of the United States came
many settlers who were good people and learned to live in
peace with the Indians of the prairie country. But as more
and more covered wagons rolled along the trails, the search
for land grew feverish and there were some who turned evil
eyes on the land where stood the tepees and the council
fires of the Comanche." (Sound effects: hoofbeats) Two of

the evil-eyed bad men are Monty and Spur, who have found some Indian land they plan to grab and sell to the settlers. They ride to meet the other desperadoes, who are decked out in war paint and Indian clothes. The band raids the homes of settlers and sets them afire, so that the Comanches will be blamed. After a Nabisco commercial, the announcer narrates: "Monty and his gang, dressed as Indians, made one night raid after another. Outlying settlers living near Comanche territory awoke night after night to hear the thunder of hoofs, the hiss of arrows, and the crack of rifle bullets, and the crackle of flames as the raiding parties burned down their homes." (This narrative is accompanied by the appropriate sound effects.) Steve and his old sidekick, Packy, are talking about the raids--they know the Comanches are innocent. There is a meeting scheduled with a judge from Washington, so Steve and Packy ride to the town to tell the man, Judge Prentiss, that the Indians are innocent. But Monty and Spur horn in on the conversation, telling the judge the Indians are to blame. Steve becomes suspicious when he finds out Monty isn't a settler. Suddenly an Indian, White Cloud, appears! "We keep the peace." "He's lyin'!" "White Cloud does not lie." Monty draws his gun, but Steve shoots the gun from his hand, and they help White Cloud escape. Steve and Packy ride to the ranch, to--"A mysterious valley, a hidden cave known only to Steve Adams and Packy. Its walls glitter with gold, and in the cave stands the great golden palomino, Fury! The Comanche bow and arrows hang on the wall. There is Comanche war paint, Comanche garb! In a moment, Steve Adams, rancher, is gone--and in his place--" "Steady, Fury, it is I--Straight Arrow!" They ride for the council fires of the Comanches, where the braves are talking about fighting for their land. They have heard of Straight Arrow, and they ask him what they should do.

Straight Arrow, who wears the red feather headband of the Comanche, tells them he will find out who is guilty. Meanwhile, Monty and Spur are plotting to convince Judge Prentiss, who's "too honest." The judge is staying at Carson's ranch, so they decide to stage a raid while the judge is there. Straight Arrow and Packy ride into town; discovering where the men are meeting, they overhear them discussing the plot. Monty hears a noise outside, but Straight Arrow and Packy make a clean getaway with the men shooting at them. Straight Arrow goes into the general store and comes out with a heavy sack which he gives to Packy to carry on his horse; he tells Packy to follow the gang as they ride out of town, while he goes for White Cloud and the other Comanches. Straight Arrow tells the braves about the plot, and they all put on their war paint and the red feather headbands. But how will they find the men who want to steal their land? How will they find the trail in the dark? The outlaws gathered at the Carson ranch, but before Monty could give the command to begin the raid the Comanches, led by Straight Arrow, ride down on them! All the outlaws are captured, and Straight Arrow leads them up to the porch. Judge Prentiss says, "So--so this is what has been happening, eh? It was not the Comanche who were raiding innocent settlers." Straight Arrow replies, "No, Judge Prentiss--it was these bad men. They hoped to get the Indian land for themselves, to sell." The judge assures the Comanches the land is theirs. We find out that the sack Straight Arrow gave Packy was full of flour. He cut the sack, so that Packy would leave a trail of flour as he followed the outlaws. Straight Arrow explains to the judge that only the Comanche wear the red feather headband; all others are fakes. After a Nabisco Shredded Wheat commercial, we hear Straight Arrow, "Faster, Palomino! Faster, Fury!" The announcer concludes: "For thrilling adventures of the old West, ride with *Straight Arrow!* And remember--(the Indian tom-tom drums begin) N-A-B-I-S-C-O, Nabisco is the name to know. For a breakfast you can't beat, try Nabisco Shredded Wheat!"

This episode of *Straight Arrow* was typical of the series, in its portrayal of the Red Man as noble and peace-loving, and always truthful. However, the dialogue for the Indians (especially Straight Arrow) was stilted and trite, and there was nothing unusual or original about the plot. There were plenty of sound effects and lots of action, and the voices made it easy to tell the characters apart. The *Rin Tin Tin* episode featured far more imaginative Indian dialogue, which would have made the Red Man seem much more likeable and real to the young listeners. This *Straight Arrow* episode leaned more heavily on the use of narration to explain the story than did the other Children's Hour programs of the late 1940's and early 1950's. By that time, most of the writers had learned to carry the story line with dialogue. *Straight Arrow* may have been shot down by poor scripting.

TENNESSEE JED

This show was a frontier adventure 15-minute serial with Tennessee Jed Sloan and his horse Smoky after the bad men five days a week on ABC from 1945 until 1947. Tennessee was supposed to be a super marksman, and was one of the very few Children's Hour heroes who had no sidekick to talk to. MacDonald (1979) wrote that this led to the program's demise because of a lack of humor (the hero was usually dead serious in radio Westerns) (p. 198). However, the most successful Western of them all, *The Lone Ranger,* was almost totally devoid of humor; certainly Tonto wasn't a comic relief partner.

The episode of January 22, 1946, began with a yodel and a sustained high note under, "There he goes, Tennessee! Git him!" A gunshot and its ricochet is next, "Got him! Deaaaad center!" Then the yodeling resumes, followed by, "That's Jed Sloan, *Tennessee Jed,* deadliest man with a rifle ever to ride the western plains, brought to you every day, Monday through Friday, by the bakers of enriched Tip Top Bread. Nick Dalton plans to renew the war between the states and take over the government. So, by clever lying he provokes a group of Del Rio men to attack Federal troops coming from San Antonio as replacements for those killed in his recent raid on Camp Hudson. Tennessee and Snake attempt to capture Dalton before the battle takes place and fail. Then Cookstove, Sheriff Tate and José meet up with what they believe to be the Del Rio advance guard, only to learn too late the group is headed by Dalton himself--and they wind up with hangman's nooses around their necks." Cookstove says he's entitled to last words, before he "swings in the breeze" (Dalton's sneering words). He says Dalton will never get away with it, especially hanging a sheriff. But Dalton reveals his plan--to leave them hanging from the tree, and when the Del Rio rear guard comes, they will think it was done by their enemies, and a war will start. This would put Dalton in charge when the government is overthrown. We are left hanging (figuratively) while the announcer returns with a commercial for Tip Top Bread. The theme music comes in--guitar, with the yodeling. When the story returns, Dalton gives the order to slap the horses to hang the three men, but we hear Tennessee's yodel--then three gunshots (complete with ricochets) as he shoots the ropes, breaking them. Dalton escapes as Tennessee and Snake ride to see about Cookstove, the sheriff and José, who regains consciousness first--Snake remarks, "He's one tough Mexicano." José replies, "Sí--in old Mexico there ees no man so tough than José Rosito--or Texas too--I never mees!" Snake points out that Tennessee never misses either and it's a good thing he didn't. But Tennessee attributes it to luck, the kind provided only by the Lord. When the sheriff comes to, he thinks he's in heaven. Cookstove tells them that Dalton is on his way to Shreveport to spread the word that there's war in Texas, so the troups will leave for Texas and allow Dalton to take over Louisiana. Tennessee's plan is to stop the Del Rio group from attacking the troops, so Dalton's plan will fail. The bridge is provided by a song from Tennessee, accompanied by guitar. "Stoppin' fightin' means much more than catchin' ol' Nick Dalton." The announcer returns, "Will Tennessee be able to talk the Del Rio group out of fighting and avert a head-on battle with Federal troops? We'll see in just 60 seconds!" Then comes another Tip Top commercial, followed by more yodeling. "Tennessee has only a short wait, for even now the Del Rio rear guard is approaching the spot where Cookstove, the sheriff and José came so close to death." We hear the sound of marching feet, and the officer asks who they are. "They calls me Tennessee." The officer introduces himself as a major in the Confederate Army. Tennessee asks, "Yer kinda fergittin', ain't ya, Major--war is over." The major asks, "Are you friend or foe?" Tennessee replies, "Friend of the Yew-nited States, Major--and foe to all what plots against her!" Tennessee tells him about Dalton's plot, but the major is convinced the Federal troops are coming to put the country under military rule. He tells them they are prisoners, and his marksmen will wipe out the Federal troops. The announcer comes in for the conclusion: "Oh, oh! Instead of winning over Major Deveraux, Tennessee is made a prisoner to be dealt with after the first battle of another war between the states! This is Lehman Cameron, gang, asking you to be sure to listen again tomorrow at this same time to the next exciting chapter in the thrilling adventures of-- (yodel with sustained high note under)--*Tennessee Jed!* (Sound effects: gunshot with ricochet). The stars say it's better bread! Look for the star-end wrapper for delicious and enriched Tip Top Bread today! This is ABC, the American Broadcasting Company."

The serial had a somewhat different sound to it, mostly because of the yodeling and guitar music bridges (presumably Tennessee yodeled wherever he rode.) There were plenty of good sound effects, but a bit more reliance on the narrator than in some of the other later programs. Tennessee's accent sounded appropriately Southern-frontier, José's accent definitely Mexican, and Cookstove had the old cowhand's voice. There was plenty of action, and parents must have approved of Tennessee's apparent religiousness and patriotism--but they probably didn't approve much of the detailed description of how to hang a man at the first of the show. The cliffhanger ending was fairly mild. This time the hero is merely taken prisoner rather than being in a life-threatening situation. Although Tennessee might not have had a regular sidekick, he sure had plenty of company in this particular episode.

TERRY AND THE PIRATES

Milton Caniff's comic strip character, Terry Lee, came to radio in 1937 on NBC. *Terry and the Pirates* faced unspeakable dangers in the Orient daily for two years. The show went off the air until 1943, when it returned, a natural because now Terry and his friends, Patrick Ryan, Hot Shot Charlie, the Chinese giant Big Stoop, Connie the Coolie, and the lovely Burma could fight the Axis in the Orient. During the hiatus, a movie serial was produced by Columbia in 1940. *Terry and the Pirates* was one of the first Children's Hour shows to fight fascism, and some thought the show built understanding of people of the Orient. Terry's running battle was with the exotic Dragon Lady (sometimes played by Agnes Moorhead), but an uneasy truce was drawn during the war with the Dragon Lady also fighting the enemy. *Terry and the Pirates* went off the air in 1948, and returned on television from 1952 through 1953.

"Quaker Puffed Wheat Sparkies bring you-- (Sound effects: Gong, followed by Chinese-sounding music, and someone speaking in Chinese)--*Terr--eee and the Pirates!"* In the episode broadcast December 14, 1947, the narrator begins: "Terry and two of his friends, Hot Shot and the Chinese giant Big Stoop have driven by car to lonely Tung Lake in search of the stolen Mechanical Eye. They're pretending to be on a fishing vacation, and have told the tough owner of a ramshackle lakeside hotel they're up from Hong Kong. This hotel has some odd things about it, including Trigger Goo and his mother. There's a savage wolf dog, for instance, and the strange odor of photographic chemicals. And in just a moment, you'll get in on a new midnight clue with this new adventure of the Mechanical Eye. So stand by!" (Sound effects: gong) After a singing commercial for Quaker Puffed Wheat Sparkies ("Here comes Quaker with a bang-bang.") "Terry and his two pals came to Tung Lake, some two or three hundred miles inland from Hong Kong. Because a plane was said to be there--a plane equipped with a stolen invention known as the Mechanical Eye. And now Terry, Charlie and Big Stoop are in the Goo Hotel, in a dimly lit room. They've trapped Baldo, the savage wolf dog, tied him up and muffled his snarls. And now as they prepare to investigate the hotel at this midnight hour, a new sound reaches Terry--it's an outboard motor--"One of those motors you attach to a rowboat." Maybe Trigger is expecting visitors! Then Trigger comes looking for his dog, whom they have hidden under Big Stoop's bed. The dog whines, and Big Stoop pretends to be sick and groans. Strange--his groans sounded like a dog whining! Trigger leaves, and they see a man coming up the path from the lake carrying a heavy suitcase. The Mechanical Eye? Perhaps they've brought it here to develop the film taken by the eye; they know, of course, a darkroom is here because of the smell of the chemicals. Later they sneak downstairs looking for the darkroom, and they hear Trigger talking to the man about the delivery. "Wow! That does it, Charlie. We're gettin' mighty close to the Mechanical Eye!" After a commercial, the narrator says, *"Terry and the Pirates* is dramatized for radio by Albert Barker who says: Terry is right. The stolen Mechanical Eye is linked with Trigger Goo, and the answer is here at Tung Lake. But will our friends find the darkroom without being caught? That's on deck for tomorrow, same time, same station. *Terry and the Pirates* is directed by Martin Andrews, and is heard overseas through the Armed Forces Radio Service." (Sound effects: Gong, followed by Chinese music.)

Another episode (date unknown, but probably earlier, due to the slightly different introduction) begins with: "Quaker Puffed Wheat is shot from guns! (bang, bang) Quaker Puffed Rice is shot from guns! (bang, bang) After the commercial, we hear, "And now, Quaker Puffed Wheat and Quaker Puffed Rice bring you--(Sound effects: gong, and Chinese music)--*Terr-eee and the Pirates,* the new and exciting adventure of Terry Lee and the Pirate's Gold Detector Ring!" Terry has been captured by the Khan, and is pleading with the Khan to release him so he can find the ring, but the Khan is adamant in his belief that Terry has the ring. Terry is convinced that Turnbull has it, but the Khan tells him, "Unless the ring is returned before the full moon, a curse will fall upon us all." Meanwhile, in Shanghai, Pat, Hot Shot and Burma are wondering where Terry is, after he and Connie escaped from jail. Burma is unhappy with Pat because he hasn't found Terry yet. Pat has found a box of American cough drops in the house where Chung Fu was murdered; they happen to be the brand Turnbull uses. Burma takes them, and leaves for her dangerous rendezvous with Turnbull. Hot Shot tells Pat, "What a gal! They don't come any braver, do they?" The next scene finds a long, low convertible driving through the country outside of Shanghai. Burma and Turnbull (who puffs a cigarette through a long ivory holder) are in the back seat. Turnbull asks Burma if she is worried about Terry Lee, but she pretends to be unconcerned and asks Turnbull to tell her about himself. He does, interspersed by coughing. She hands him the box of cough drops. "I found them in a dark little house." Turnbull understands; he wants to get out of the country, and she wants the ring. The narrator says, "Well--it looks like Burma played her hand just right, doesn't it? Turnbull didn't admit much about those lozenges, but it isn't hard to see he's getting crowded into a rather dangerous corner. Do you think he will now show Burma the Pirate Gold Detector Ring? And meanwhile, what of Terry, whose whole future seems to depend on the whereabouts of that ring? In a moment, we'll hear the Khan tell Terry a very strange thing!" After a commercial, the Khan tells Terry he has learned of Burma and Turnbull's meeting, and urges Terry to "produce the ring and save yourself, my son, save yourself!" The conclusion: "While Pat and Hot Shot scramble to gather facts that will help Terry and Connie, Terry, trapped, helpless, faces the eleventh hour. Listen tomorrow! *Terry and the Pirates* is written by Harrison Bingham, and is brought you each day, Monday through Friday, same time, same station. So listen tomorrow when Quaker Puffed Wheat and Quaker Puffed Rice bring you--(Sound effects: Gong, followed by Chinese music)--*Terr---eee and the Pirates!"*

Terry and the Pirates was full of dark and mysterious happenings in a strange land; fascinating to the youngsters who could identify with the youthful Terry. Of course, the requisite cliffhanger endings kept them coming back, day after day, to find out what might happen to Terry and his friends. The shows were typical of the serial format, in that the plot was drawn out and there was actually very little real action happening. The voice characterizations were well done, and the sound effects plentiful. The opening sound montage was particularly effective in setting the scene, conjuring up visions of crowded streets and coolies pulling rickshaws. The exotic locale was at least partly reponsible for the program's popularity.

TOM CORBETT, SPACE CADET

This story of 24th Century Earth was a latecomer to radio; it ran on television at the same time, and also appeared in the comics. Tom Corbett was a cadet at Space Academy, where he and his friends Astro and Roger Manning were in training to become Solar Guards. Tom first appeared on television in 1950, then on ABC radio in January of 1952, lasting slightly less than a year.

An episode dated January 15, 1952, began with: "Kellogg's Pep, the build-up cereal, invites you to rocket into the future with *Tom Corbett, Space Cadet.* Stand by to blast off! Five, four, three, two, one, zero! (Sound effects: rockets blasting off) As roaring rockets blast off to distant planets and far flung stars, we take you to the age of the conquest of space with *Tom Corbett, Space Cadet!*" After the theme music, the story begins with a distress call from Captain Parker in a rocket scout ship. The chief asks Captain Strong if his cadets can handle a rescue operation, but the cadets have been called on the carpet for fighting. The skipper gets them off to take the rescue mission, and Tom, Astro and Roger Manning blast off in the Polaris to search through the asteroid belt. Astro (the Venusian) and Roger are still mad at each other. They dodge asteroids (risky business indeed), and are hit by a meteor which takes out their communications. They slow to an orbit to make repairs outside the ship, when Roger Manning is hit by a meteor and cast adrift from the ship! After a commercial, Captain Strong tells Astro to bring out a body jet, but Astro tells them there isn't enough time, and he expertly maneuvers the ship to pick Roger up. Roger is appropriately grateful, and the cadets bury the hatchet. The announcer concludes by telling us to tune Thursday for the conclusion.

That episode, dated January 17, 1952, begins with the same opening. The theme music comes up, then, "Attention crew! Attention crew! We are clear of the asteroid belt--resume scatter watch for Captain Parker and the missing rocket scout! Attention crew! Attention crew--(fades out). Manned by Captain Strong and his crew of space cadets, the rocket Polaris blasts through the blackness of the void, combing millions of miles of empty space for the missing rocket scout 4J9, unreported for almost three days. On the control deck, Tom Corbett and his skipper guide their powerful ship on an erratic search orbit, tracking down every target on the radar scanners, checking every wandering meteor. But as the hours pass, the search seems to grown more and more hopeless, and the reports from Roger Manning on the radar bridge topside become more and more discouraging." Roger says the sector they are searching has been completely covered, and the skipper tells Astro to alter course. They receive a message from headquarters ordering them to abandon the search, when suddenly, a blip appears on the radar screen! It's a jet boat, and it has to be from the rocket scout! Tom and the skipper don their space suits and get into their jet boat to go have a look. They come up alongside the jet boat and use the magnetic couplers. They open the portals and go over to the other jet boat, only to find it empty! "Then what happened to Captain Parker?" Next comes a commercial for Kellogg's Pep, which begins with the sound of a jet plane and urges the kids to keep themselves in shape for the future (so they can become jet pilots) by eating Kellogg's Pep. We return to the story, and find that the jet boat has been jettisoned by Captain Parker in hopes that they would find it. A note, dated four days earlier, informs them that Rocket Scout 4J9 has been hit by a meteor and has had to land on Jupiter--"the worst planet in the solar system." They return to the Polaris, although neither of them believes that Parker could survive four days on Jupiter, where there are storms and sub-freezing temperatures. Suddenly Roger receives a weak radio signal from Jupiter! They go in closer, where the signal indicates the ship may be right below them. The skipper calls the cadets on the intercom to give them the facts so they can decide what to do. Roger wants to go down and get them, but the skipper says, "Now let me tell you a few things about Jupiter first, Manning. Even though it's a giant planet, it whirls on its axis like a top. Now this action creates storms that make our hurricanes on Earth seem like spring breezes." He tells them the days are only six hours long, and when night comes the temperature is so cold they would have only 20 minutes before freezing. Also the gravity is two-and-a-half times that of Earth and the atmosphere is filled with noxious gases. Nonetheless, the courageous cadets vote to go down. After landing, they get only static on the radio, so they put on their thermal suits and masks and go out onto the surface to search for the rocket scout. It is very difficult to walk because of the gravity--on Jupiter, they each weigh about 450 pounds. They find the rocket scout and enter. Parker is alive but unconscious, and they try, with great difficulty, to carry him back to the Polaris. Suddenly they see that a nearby mountain appears to be exploding--it's an earthquake! Next is a commercial, with a premium offer--a "Magic Moving Picture Eye," one of the cards held in the hand that has a picture that moves when the card is rotated. When we return to the story, the crew is trying to walk on the heaving surface of Jupiter, with chasms opening up around them. They make it to the Polaris, and blast off. Tom says, "Goodbye, Jupiter. If I ever see you again, it'll be through a telescope!" The announcer concludes: "Don't miss the next action-packed adventure with *Tom Corbett and the Space Cadets* on Tuesday, when danger and death strike from the void, in the 'Mystery of the Space Station of Danger.' (Music sting) Tune in same time, same station for the next thrilling interplanetary adventure with (echo) *Tom Corbett, Space Cadet.* (Sound effects: rocket blasting off) Brought to you by Kellogg's Pep, the build-up wheat cereal. (The theme music comes up.) *Tom Corbett, Space Cadet,* starring Frankie Thomas, can also be seen on television and appears in the comic sections of many of America's leading newspapers. Look for it daily and in weekend editions. Featured in the cast are Al Markim as

Astro, Jan Merlin as Roger Manning, and Edward Brice as Captain Strong. Today's program was written by Jack Weinstock and Willie Gilbert, directed by Drex Hines. Jackson Beck speaking." Another commercial, this time for Kellogg's Raisin Bran, follows.

The program was another typical of the later shows, which probably would have had longer runs had they not been competing with television. The two episodes were filled with sound effects and plenty of technical descriptions of space ships and the planets to satisfy any child curious about outer space. The voices were a bit difficult to distinguish, and the cadets sounded quite mature, but the dialogue was snappy and filled with wisecracks from Roger and Astro. The 30-minute episodes were likely typical of the show's format--a story beginning on Tuesday and concluding on Thursday. Parents would have been pleased with the educational aspects of this episode, and the lack of mayhem.

THE TOM MIX
RALSTON STRAIGHTSHOOTERS

The Tom Mix Ralston Straightshooters was one of the longest-running children's adventures on radio. It began on NBC in 1933, and ended on Mutual in 1950. During the majority of its run, the show was a 15-minute serial, but in the last year, it became a 30-minute feature, with each episode a complete story. The earlier shows were introduced and narrated by the Old Wrangler, who was later replaced by an announcer. The real Tom Mix, who was well known in the movies, never appeared on the radio, and the episodes ended with the information that "Tom Mix was impersonated." This was fortunate, because the western star was killed in an auto accident in 1940, but

the radio show continued 10 years after his death. Tom
Mix was another of the cowboy characters who came from
the movies to radio. Tom returned to the film in 1935 for
his only serial, *The Miracle Rider*. Tom Mix's sponsor
for most of the run was Ralston, and mothers, who may not
have loved the general mayhem on the show, did approve
of the product, a hot cereal. On the other hand, the young
Straightshooters may not have loved eating Ralston, but
they did love the premiums that could be obtained with a
few boxtops and perhaps a dime. Among the prizes were a
compass-magnifying glass, flashlights, telescopes, pocket
knives, badges, sound transmitters, rings, codebooks, safety
spurs that could be seen in the dark, and the Tom Mix
Movie Make-up Kit (Churchhill, 1967).

During the war, Tom joined the other characters of
the Children's Hour in fighting the Axis. This was,
however, usually restricted to keeping Dobie, Texas (home
of the TM-Bar Ranch) safe from the enemy.

One of the wartime episodes used the enemy spy
theme, but had Tom leaving the ranch for this mystery.
The quarter-hour episode, broadcast May 8, 1945 (V-E
Day), began with the announcer: "*The Tom Mix Ralston
Straightshooters* are on the air! And here comes Tom Mix,
America's favorite cowboy, with another thrill packed
Western adventure program." (Sound effects: horse
whinnying and hoofbeats) Tom cries, "Come on, boy!"
Then, although Tom Mix wasn't known as a singing
cowboy, the latest radio Tom Mix (Curley Bradley)
followed with the Ralston song, "Shredded Ralston for your
breakfast, start the day off shinin' bright, gives you lots of
cowboy energy, with a flavor that's just right. It's delicious
and nutritious, bite size and ready to eat. Take a tip from
Tom, go and tell your mom, shredded Ralston can't be
beat!" The announcer returns with: "*The Tom Mix Ralston*

Straightshooters bring you action, mystery and mile-a-minute thrills on radio's biggest western detective program. (Music sting) Tonight you're about to hear-- (music sting) another episode in a baffling mystery--'Secret Mission'! (Music up) Tom Mix has agreed to undertake a dangerous secret mission, from which he may never return. Right now, Tom and Charles Mike Shaw find themselves in a strange city, after the plane in which they took off from the Twin Rivers Airport near Dobie was grounded because of bad weather. With them is a man who calls himself 'Mr. Moonlight.' A moment ago, another car, driven by a beautiful young woman, ran into the car in which Tom, Charles Mike and Mr. Moonlight were riding. The young lady's car was so badly wrecked that they agreed to take her home in their car. In a moment, strange and baffling things are going to happen. But first, here is Tom Mix." Tom talks about the end of part of the war, but urges the kids to keep right on buying and saving War Stamps. "And now, let's join Tom and Charles Mike, as they ride along in the rear seat of a car driven by the mysterious, white-bearded Mr. Moonlight. Seated between our friends is a tall and extraordinarily beautiful girl named Drucilla Drake." Charles Mike (who is usually called just "Mike") is trying to figure out what is happening, for it is apparent that Drucilla and Mr. Moonlight know each other. Tom informs him that it's obvious that the girl and Moonlight are trying to throw someone off their trail. They are being followed! Tom also tells Mike they are headed for Europe, because there's some dangerous folks there, even after V-E Day. Drucilla tells them the collision was planned, to throw the enemy agents off the trail. Mike thinks they should stop the car and shoot it out with the spies, but Tom tells him that's not their job. Their job is to follow orders given by K-12, even though it may cost their lives. They all agree. Meanwhile, we hear K-12 talking on the phone and instructing a pilot to land a plane just south of Drucilla Drake's house. He is informed that Mike Shaw is along; he says that Shaw is an excellent man, as long as he doesn't know too much. He tells the agent to inform the others, then Shaw after he has boarded the plane. We join our friends, who are at a party at Drucilla Drake's house. Tom points out that the party is to throw off the enemy agents--Miss Drake and Moonlight have already disappeared. Mike has been looking for her, having been smitten by her beauty. As he is talking to Tom, suddenly Tom disappears, and an Asian-sounding man hands Mike a glass of punch. He tells Mike to saunter out a door with the glass onto a terrace, and to keep walking straight. Mike does so, and walks toward a grove of trees where he hears a plane! Tom calls to him, and they board the plane with Drucilla and Moonlight. The music comes up, and the announcer says, "As the plane, with sealed orders from K-12, takes off from the airfield next to Drucilla Drake's house, something has gone wrong! One look at the face of the pilot of that plane, a face seen in the faint light of the instrument panel, will reveal a cruel looking man, with a hard, vicious smile playing about his lips. Tomorrow, thrilling and unexpected things happen. For action and rip-roaring adventure, don't miss *Tom Mix and His Ralston Straightshooters* tomorrow, in the next exciting episode of 'Secret Mission.' And now, here is Tom Mix." Tom returns to talk some more about the continued war effort to defeat Japan; and the part the kids can play by buying War Stamps and War Bonds until there is no more war anywhere. The Ralston theme music comes up, and the announcer concludes: "*The Tom Mix Straightshooters* were brought to you by the makers of Shredded Ralston, regular Ralston and Instant Ralston. Tom Mix was played by Curley

Bradley. Don Gordon speaking. This is the Mutual Broadcasting System."

The episode broadcast December 16, 1949, fell within the show's final year, and was one of the complete-in-30 minutes scripts. The show opens with organ music that simulates galloping horses. Announcer Don Gordon tells us, "*The Ralston Straightshooters* are on the air! And from out of the West comes Tom---m Mix, America's favorite cowboy!" Tom follows, singing the Ralston song with the words slightly changed for hot Ralston cereal. The announcer returns with: "Tonight--the makers of Ralston, the Straightshooter cereal, bring you Tom Mix, United States Marshall, in the 'Myster--ee of the Magic Mesa!'" We join Tom and his deputy, Mike Shaw, and Tom's employee, Wash, at a cattlemen's meeting, where they meet a new rancher named Ringo O'Rourke. Right away, we are suspicious of him--good guys in the West aren't named "Ringo." They hear a commotion in the street--the old prospector has come down from the mesa, spooked by seeing a ghost--Wild Bill Crockett, a giant of a man who has been dead for ten years. Wash is certainly upset by this news, but Tom tries to reassure him: "There's no such thing as ghosts. You oughta know that." Wash replies, "Yeah, ah knows it--but does de ghostes knows it?" Then mysterious lights appear on the mesa! There's something there--if not a ghost, then what was it? Tom is ready--"That's something I aim to find out. Let's get our horses, Mike! We're ridin' for the mesa, pronto!" After a commercial, we hear the bad guys talking up on the mesa, and learn that the ghost is actually Wild Bill's brother, Jack; a mentally deficient-sounding oaf who doesn't like being compared to his brother. "He was a chicken-livered coward, compared to me. Compared to me, Wild Bill was so small he could sleep in his hat! Me, I'm

tough--tougher'n my dead brother ever was!" He keeps
complaining because they haven't given him any steak.
The rest of the gang of smugglers, Ringo and Swayback,
discuss the problem with their plan to scare away any
ranchers who might come to the mesa to hunt, but they
didn't count on Mix! They see Tom approaching on the
trail below--"We're dry-gulchin' Mix and Shaw!" As Tom,
Mike and Wash approach, they have figured out that the
smugglers are involved. Suddenly, gunshots! "They got us
pinned down in the crossfire! (Sound effects: rifle shot,
blood-curdling scream) They *had* us pinned down, you
mean--that's one gone!" "Yeah, nice shootin', Tom!" After
Tom shoots the rifle from Ringo's hands, and renders
Crockett unconscious by "laying a bullet alongside his
skull" (thus keeping the giant from ripping them apart with
his bare hands), we learn that Swayback isn't dead, or even
injured badly enough to prevent his being locked up in the
jail. It takes both sets of handcuffs to make sure Jack
Crockett doesn't break loose--"all body and absolutely no
brains." Safely locked up, Jack keeps yelling for steak, and
throws his plate of breakfast at the sheriff. Ringo and
Swayback (fully recovered) incite Jack to break out of the
jail, because there's steak at the hotel down the street. Jack
breaks down the wall, but doesn't bother with Ringo and
Swayback. "Running amuck, the great giant of a man, Jack
Crockett, crushes his way toward the street--and tragedy! In
a moment, a climax you'll never forget!" After the
commercial, we find Tom in the gunsmith's shop, where
(in a uncharacteristic lapse of good judgment) he leaves
both his guns to be repaired. Tom comes face-to-face with
the rampaging Jack, who vows, "I'm agonna bust ya in
two--throw me in jail and starve me, will ya?" Tom wins
the fight through the use of brains and his skill as a fighter
(but only after being thrown through a plate-glass window).

We leave Tom heading for the hotel and a steak--not to eat, for his black eye! "And so, after one of the greatest fights of his career, Marshall Tom Mix brings to a successful close the 'Mystery of the Magic Mesa!' (Commercial) And say--be sure to listen to Tom Mix Friday for (Music sting) the 'Mystery of Panther Pass,' a story of rip-roaring western adventure. Tom Mix was played by Curley Bradley, and written by George Lowther. The part of Deputy Mike Shaw was played by Leo Curlee." Tom's Ralston song is repeated, and the announcer concludes with, "This is Don Gordon, speaking for Ralston, the hot whole wheat cereal that's mightly good tasting and mighty good for you."

This later episode was perhaps more typical in theme to the shows broadcast before the war, with Tom fighting Old West-type bad guys on or near the ranch. The programs were popular because of the action and the mystery angle. Although there was lots of shooting, no one was actually killed, and injuries were shrugged off. In fact, this was a trademark of all *Tom Mix* stories, including the movies, that no one was ever killed. The dialogue was snappy, and marked by typical stereotyping of voices, the worst of which was the voice of Wash, Tom's cook, handyman, and sometimes detective. In the land of juvenile (and adult) radio, blacks were often humorous characters; their dialogue was full of bad grammar, and Wash, although included in the adventure, was constantly mumbling about how scared he was. Women, of course, were few and far between in the Wild West of Tom Mix, appearing occasionally to be rescued.

UNCLE DON

There were quite a few radio "Uncles," early-day children's program hosts who thrived at the local level.

The best-known of them all was the WOR Uncle, Don
Carney, and part of his fame was due to something he
likely didn't say. A *Time* article in October of 1939
reported that he would probably pay a good part of his
$20,000 yearly salary to be rid of the persistent tale that he
said, at the end of the broadcast when he thought he was off
the air, "There! I guess that'll hold the little bastards!"
("Snork, punk," 1939, p. 64). MacDonald (1979), in
Don't Touch That Dial!, wrote that the infamous line was
actually uttered by a Philadelphia children's show host,
Uncle Wip of WIP, in 1930. The hapless Uncle Wip was
fired for his faux pas (p. 43). Uncle Don joined WOR in
1925, and did an impromptu children's show for a toy
manufacturer in 1928. This evolved into his standard
format, which included stories, songs, jokes, various clubs
(having to do with his sponsors' products), advice against
misbehaving, and birthday greetings. The last was
described in *Newsweek* (1949). "If little Jackie Smith of
such-and-such Blank Avenue will just look behind the
pillows of Mother's bedroom chair he will find a nice
birthday present there" ("Uncle Don's," 1940, p. 52). The
children, unaware of the collaboration between Mother and
Uncle Don, thought he was magic. His loyal young
audience knew the meanings of Uncle Don's made-up
words that described unacceptable behavior: "crytearian,
fakerup, romeroff, scuffyheeler, leavearounder, and
muddlerup" (LaCerda, 1946, p. 17). But, in spite of the
innocuous nature of the show, all parents weren't crazy
about Don. A *Scribner's Magazine* writer said that his
"shortcoming is driving parents almost to distraction with
the monotony of procedure and tiresome plugs" (Mann,
1933, p. 315). One parent thought that Uncle Don seemed
too juvenile even for juveniles. The young listeners were
automatically "club members"--bound to buy the products

advertised--candy, toys, books, chocolate drink powder. His opening song was filled with nonsense words: "Hello, nephews, nieces too. Mothers and daddies, how are you? This is Uncle Don, all set to go with a meeting on the radio. We'll start off with a little song; to learn the words will not take long. For they're easy as easy can be, so come on now, and sing with me. Hibbidy gits has ha ring boree, honikodoke with an alikazon, sing this song with your Uncle Don." This went on six nights a week, Monday through Saturday, from 1929 until 1949, so it appears the children and the sponsors liked him, even if he did drive grown-ups frantic. (The show was heard on Mutual for a brief time in 1939.)

The program of August 10, 1945, was notable because of the rumored end of World War II. Uncle Don begins with, "Hello, boys and girls--it's your Uncle Don. Yes sir, we're all ready for a club meeting, too, and I'm just as excited as you are, I betcha! Well, I say excited--I'm anxious--I wanta hear that good news that we hope is going to come through after a little bit." He talks about the hoped-for news that the war was over, and how he figures that maybe the Japanese did have some brains after all. He goes on about how bad war was, and how great it would be to get back to normal--no rationing, drive our cars to a picnic. He tells the kids that we'll have to help the people who were invaded, and how awful it must have been. Finally, he plays the piano and sings the opening song, followed by the Pledge of Allegiance. Then he talks about the weather, and gives some birthday greetings to several children. His "club meeting" is mentioned only briefly, and concludes by touting his appearance at Palisades Park, asking the kids to write in for free tickets, and signs off with, "Bye now."

Certainly this was not a typical Uncle Don show,

but no others were located that would contain the stories that were more the norm, with his characters Willipus Wallipus, Suzan Beduzin and her brother Huzen, or his admonitions to "brush your teeth" and not throw tantrums. If this particular episode had been typical, it's doubtful Uncle Don would have been around for as long as he was--kids would have been pretty bored with a 15-minute one-sided conversation. Uncle Don (whose real name was Howard Rice) also read the Sunday Hearst comics over the air, and hosted a show called *Dog Chat,* which featured stories about dogs.

WILD BILL HICKOK

This 30-minute tale of the Old West came on Mutual December 31, 1951, and ran until 1956. Wild Bill and his sidekick Jingles P. Jones simultaneously fought the bad guys on television in 1952, and returned to TV in 1957-1958. The stories were set in the Southwest in the 1870's, where U.S. Marshall Hickok (played by Guy Madison) and Jingles (played by Andy Devine) had their adventures.

An undated episode began with, "*Wild Bill Hickok,* transcribed in Hollywood, and starring Guy Madison as Wild Bill, and Andy Devine as his pal Jingles. In just 30 seconds you'll hear the exciting story, 'Cave-in at Careful Smith's Mine.'" After a commercial, "On the long procession of pioneers who traversed our broad continent pushinhg the early frontiers ever westward, most were honest, law-abiding. But some were not, and the battle between the good and the bad was often violent. Into this conflict, always on the side of law and order, rode the greatest fighter of them all--scout, sharpshooter, United States Marshall--Wild Bill Hickok! Early one evening, in the town of Silver City, two men sat together in the corner shadows of the Cactus Bed Saloon, and they spoke quietly." One of the men, Adam Cobb, has sent for the other, Stacey. They discuss what has transpired: Cobb, who is the boss, provides grubstakes for prospectors. Then when the prospectors strike it rich, they meet with an accident (like Careful Smith who died in a cave-in) and Cobb gets the mine. But old Jim Harris, who knows something is afoot, has sent for Wild Bill, so Stacey is dispatched to see that Harris gets a case of "lockjaw--permanent lockjaw." Wild Bill and Jingles are riding to meet Jim Harris, when a shot rings out! Harris has been shot, and with his last dying breath, he tells them that Careful Smith's death wasn't an accident. Wild Bill and Jingles ride to the sheriff, but he is convinced that Smith's death was an accident. Cobb, who is a lawyer, comes in and tells them that Smith had an argument with another prospector named Sourdough. Wild Bill and Jingles are going to find Sourdough, when someone throws a knife at them! The knife has a note attached to it, signed "The Bushwacker," and it warns them to leave Silver City or get the same as Jim Harris. They can't find Sourdough, so they ride for the mine. When they get there, they see the mine was built by a careful man, and built to stand. Sourdough is there with a gun, and makes them listen--he says he didn't kill anyone and he runs from them. There is another cave-in, and they try to escape. Back in town, Cobb and Stacey have captured Sourdough and tell the sheriff that Sourdough set off the avalanche at the mine, trapping Wild Bill and Jingles. They ride for the mine to rescue the two, and after digging through to the mine, they find no one there. Then the deputy, Clem, rides up to tell them that Sourdough has diappeared from the jail! Wild Bill and Jingles have escaped the mine and have taken Sourdough, convinced of his innocence. Wild Bill and Jingles tell Sourdough they found another entrance to the mine. They have a plan to bait a trap for a murderer! After a promo for television, we return to the story. Cobb and Stacey are in Cobb's office, and suddenly someone shoots out the lamp! It is Wild Bill, and he tells Cobb and Stacey they have a witness to their crime; and that Sourdough and the sheriff are coming for them. Stacey sees Sourdough running down the street with the sheriff after him--he panics and runs, and the sheriff shoots him off his horse! Wild Bill subdues Cobb, and then tells him that there was no witness--the sheriff was chasing Sourdough, not coming to arrest them. They have been tricked! The theme music comes in, and the announcer concludes: "Another exciting story of *Wild Bill Hickok,* starring Guy Madison and Andy Devine in person. Today's cast included Hal Gerard, Jeff Kirkpatrick, Lou Marcel, Tyler McVey and Barney Phillips. Our director is Paul Pierce. Music by Dick O'Ryan. This is a David Hire Production, transcribed in Hollywood." The theme music comes up to close.

After the close, we find that the show is a re-broadcast for Armed Forces Radio, so there is no real clue as to when the show was originally broadcast. The episode was typical of the late radio shows, with good scripting, sound effects and dialogue. Certainly the presence of two actors like Madison and Devine helped the show to have a fairly long run for a late-entry radio show, considering the competition from television.

WILDERNESS ROAD

CBS tried to mollify the anti-blood-and-thunder forces with the adventure serial, *Wilderness Road.* The show was a 15-minute serialized drama of American frontier life, featuring the pioneer Weston family on the trail with Daniel Boone. Whipple (1938) documented a speech made by CBS's consulting psychologist for children's programs, Arthur T. Jersild, to the members of the Institute for Education by Radio about *Wilderness Road*. Jersild called it "an experiment in worth-while entertainment," and emphasized the fact that the shows didn't rely on the usual cliffhanger episodes. He used as an example one of the episodes in which John and David, the two oldest Weston boys, are out hunting with Bunch Flowers, "the lovable but somewhat timid and superstitious colored servant." (Another example of the stereotyped black on radio drama.) They shoot and wound a mountain lion, which charges them. This would seem like the perfect place to end the day's episode, but the writers, Charles Tazewell and Richard Stevenson, take it a step further, to avoid overstimulating suspense. A shot rings out, and John cries, "The lion's dead--we're saved--but who was it that saved us?" (pp. 330-331).

There was no tape available for *Wilderness Road;* however a script was printed in Max Wylie's 1939 book, *Radio Writing*. The programs began with the announcer: "Wilderness Road! Reliving adventurous days on the pioneer trail to Kentucky with the Weston family and Daniel Boone!" (p. 300). This episode started out with the narrator explaining that the adventurers have stopped to camp for the night by Yellow Creek. "Behind them they could see the signal smokes of the Indians--four white columns rising high in the air. Boone believes that the savages mean to seek reinforcements from other tribes before attacking the Weston party again" (p. 300). But instead of hunting Indians, Boone and the children go off in search of--soap! Boone tells the children, "We're goin' huntin'--the three of us!" Peter asks, "For bears, Uncle

Dan'l? Or mountain lions? Or venison?" Boone replies, "Nope--somethin' a lot more important than that, Peter." Peter is excited. "What? Gosh, you don't mean a buffalo?" "Nope--we're gonna hunt soap" (p. 301). The children are certainly disappointed (and probably the listeners were too), but Dan'l tells them, "Why--I s'pect you could follow the history of civilization in a bar o' soap" (p. 301). He goes on to theorize, "The tribes or folks that scrubbed themselves to a fair-you-well rubbed the most larnin' into their heads at the same time. Maybe it was because ideas can't get in through a layer o' dirt--'cause the tribes that stayed dirty is just about where they was at the beginnin'" (p. 302). They go off into the woods in search of the soapwort plant. The episode ends with Peter getting his face washed, and running after his sister Anne in an effort to wash her face. The ending narration contains considerably more suspense and excitement than the show did, "Well--if Peter catches up with Anne that young lady will undoubtedly have the cleanest face in Kentucky Territory! The Westons are happy and seemingly carefree as we leave them--but what will the morrow bring? There are many dangers in the air--and peril lurks in every thicket. We leave them, with their campfire burning bright, until tomorrow afternoon--where--at this same time--we meet again to journey down Wilderness Road!" (p. 307).

Other *Wilderness Road* episodes reportedly did have more adventure and excitement, and the show was said to be popular with parents, educators, and the youngsters. It won an award given by the Women's National Radio Committee for best children's program in 1936, its first year. *Wilderness Road* was off the air by 1937. It won awards, but no sponsors.

BIBLIOGRAPHY

Are children's radio programs a good influence? (1945, February 15). *Library Journal,* p. 175.

Atkinson, C. (1942). *Radio network contributions to education.* Boston: Meador Publishing.

Barnouw, E. (1968). *The golden web.* New York: Oxford University Press.

Bauchard, P. (1952). *The child audience: A report on press, film and radio for children.* Paris: UNESCO.

Benedict, A. E. (1935, June). A united front on children's radio programs. *Parents Magazine,* pp. 22-23, 42.

Boemer, M. L. (1984). An analysis of the violence content of the radio thriller dramas--and some comparisons with television. *Journal of Broadcasting, 28,* 341-353.

Boutell, C. B. (1941, January 11). Hi-yo, Silver lining. *The Nation,* pp. 44-45.

Braley, B. (1937, June). The children's hour--or Longfellow didn't know the half of it. *Reader's Digest,* p. 42.

Bryan, J., III (1939, October 14). Hi-yo, Silver. *Saturday Evening Post,* pp. 20-21, 131-134.

Cantril, H., & Allport, G. (1935). *The psychology of radio.* New York: Harper & Brothers.

The cereal hour. (1946, July 1). *Newsweek,* p. 80.

Chase, F., Jr. (1942). *Sound and fury.* New York: Harper & Brothers.

Child classic program competition for thrillers; prize offers banned. (1938, December 19). *Newsweek,* pp. 32, 34.

Children's Aid Society reports on survey of program preferences. (1936, February 3). *New York Times,* p. 6.

The children's hour. (1933, April 5). *The Nation,* p. 362.

The children's hour. (1947, March 24). *Time,* p. 63.

Children's radio favorites. (1936, July 11). *Publisher's Weekly,* p. 107.

Churchhill, A. (1967). *Remember when.* New York: Golden Press.

Clark, W. R. (1940). Radio listening habits of children. *Journal of Social Psychology, 12,* 131-149.

Cleaning up radio. (1933, May 18). *Business Week,* pp. 25-26.

Cookman, M. (1939, February). What do the women of America think about entertainment? *Ladies Home Journal,* pp. 20, 63.

DeBoer, J. J. (1937). The determination of children's interests in radio drama. *Journal of Applied Psychology, 21,* 456-463.

DeBoer, J. J. (1939, September 16). Radio and children's emotions. *School and Society,* pp. 369-373.

Dr. M. I. Preston's report on reactions to crime stories discussed. (1941, October 12). *New York Times,* sec. 7, p. 22.

Drabman, R. S., & Thomas, M. H. (1980). In E. L. Palmer & A. Dorr (Eds.), *Children and the faces of television.* New York: Academic Press.

Dunning, J. (1976). *Tune in yesterday.* Englewood Cliffs, NJ: Prentice-Hall.

Eisenberg, A. L. (1936). *Children and radio programs: A study of more than three thousand children in the New York metropolitan area.* New York: Columbia University Press.

Erskine, H. (1974). The polls: Causes of crime. *Public Opinion Quarterly, 38,* 287-298.

Federal Communications Commission (1975). The Mutual Broadcasting System. In L. W. Lichty & M. C. Topping (Eds.), *American broadcasting: A source book on the history of radio and television.* New York: Hastings House.

Frank, J. (1939, February). These children's programs. *Parents Magazine,* pp. 27-29, 67-69.

Frank, J. (1949). *Comics, radio, movies and children.* New York: Public Affairs Committee.

Frankel, L. (1947, April 26). In one ear. *The Nation,* p. 481.

Gerbner, G., Gross, L., Signorielli, N., Morgan, M., & Jackson-Beeck, M. (1979). *Violence profile no. 10: Trends in network television drama and viewer conceptions of social reality, 1967-1978.* Phildelphia: University of Pennsylvania.

Gibson, W. (1938, July). Radio horror: for children only. *American Mercury,* pp. 294-296.

Gilbert, J. (1986). *A cycle of outrage: America's reaction to the juvenile delinquent in the 1950s.* New York: Oxford University Press.

Gordon, D. (1942). *All children listen.* New York: George W. Stewart Publishers.

Gunther, J., & Quint, B. (1956). *Days to remember: America 1945-1955.* New York: Harper & Brothers.

Halperin, M. (1977, April 27). Telephone conversation.

Harmon, J. (1967). *The great radio heroes.* Garden City, NY: Doubleday.

Harmon, J., & Glut, D. F. (1972). *The great movie serials.* Garden City, NY: Doubleday.

Henry, T. R. (1935). "Terrorism" on the radio. *National Education Association Journal, 24,* 145-146.

Herzog, H. (1975). Why did people believe in the "invasion from Mars"? In L. W. Lichty & M. C. Topping (Eds.), *American Broadcasting: A source book on the history of radio and television.* New York: Hastings House.

Hi yo, Silver, plated. (1942, June 8). *Time,* pp. 65-66.

Houseman, J. (1972). *Run-through.* New York: Simon & Schuster.

Hutchens, J. K. (1943, November 21). Tracy, Superman, et al. go to war. *New York Times Magazine,* p. 14.

Jack, the Nazi killer. (1943, August 23). *Newsweek,* p. 80.

LaCerda, J. (1946, January 12). Anyway, the kids like them. *Saturday Evening Post,* p. 17.

Lefkowitz, M. M., & Huesmann, R. (1980). In E. L. Palmer & A. Dorr (Eds.), *Children and the faces of television.* New York: Academic Press.

Lichty, L. W. (1975). Radio drama: The early years. In L. W. Lichty & M. C. Topping (Eds.), *American broadcasting: A source book on the history of radio and television.* New York: Hastings House.

Listen, flatfoot . . . (1940, April 8). *Time,* p. 48.

Littledale, C. (1933, May). Better radio programs for children. *Parents Magazine,* p. 13.

Longstaff, H. P. (1936). Effectiveness of children's radio programs. *Journal of Applied Psychology, 20,* 208-220.

Longstaff, H. P. (1937). Mothers' opinions of children's radio programs. *Journal of Applied Psychology, 21,* 265-279.

Lundberg, G. (1975). The content of radio programs. In L. W. Lichty & M. C. Topping (Eds.), *American broadcasting: A source book on the history of radio and television.* New York: Hastings House.

MacDonald, J. F. (1979). *Don't touch that dial! Radio programming in American life, 1920-1960.* Chicago: Nelson-Hall.

Mack and the beanstalk. (1943, June 28). *Newsweek,* p. 108.

Mahlen, N. (1949, January). Comic book and other horrors: Prep school for totalitarian society? *Commentary,* pp. 80-87.

Mann, A. (1933, May 9). The children's hour of crime. *Scribner's Magazine,* pp. 313-315.

Mann, A. (1934, October). Children's crime programs: 1934. *Scribner's Magazine,* pp. 244-246.

The Masked Rider. (1952, January 14). *Time,* p. 78.

Merry, F., & Vickers, R. (1940). *From infancy to adolescence.* New York: Harper.

Mothers fighting the radio bogie. (1933, March 18). *Literary Digest,* p. 32.

Orme, F. (1978, May 8). Personal interview.

Osgood, D. (1981). *Wyxie wonderland: An unauthorized 50-year diary of WXYZ, Detroit.* Bowling Green, OH: Bowling Green University Popular Press.

Phillips, C. (1969). *The New York Times chronicle of American life: From the crash to the blitz, 1929-1939.* New York: Macmillan.

Protest: Adults condemn air hair-raisers for youngsters. (1934, December 1). *Newsweek,* p. 27.

Radio crime programs. (1940, July). *Journal of Criminal Law,* pp. 222-223.

Radio for children--parents listen in. (1933, April). *Child Study,* pp. 193-198, 214.

Radio gore criticized for making children's hour a pause that depresses. (1937. November 8). *Newsweek,* p. 26.

Schultz, G. D. (1945, November). Comics-radio-movies. *Better Homes and Gardens,* pp. 22, 73-76.

Snork, punk. (1939, October 9). *Time,* p. 64.

Spence, L. (Ed.). (1945). *Let's learn to listen.* Madison: Wisconsin Joint Committee for Better Radio Listening.

Stedman, R. W. (1971). *The serials.* Norman: University of Oklahoma Press.

Sterling, C. H., & Kittross, J. M. (1978). *Stay tuned: A concise history of American broadcasting.* Belmont, CA: Wadsworth.

Summers, H. B. (Ed.). (1939). *Radio censorship.* New York: H. W. Wilson.

Summers, H. B. (1971). *A thirty-year history of programs carried on national radio networks in the United States: 1926-1956.* New York: Arno Press & the New York Times.

Summers, R. E., & Summers, H. B. (1966). *Broadcasting and the public.* Belmont, CA: Wadsworth.

Superflight. (1946, April 29). *Newsweek,* p. 61.

Surgeon General's Scientific Advisory Committee on Television and Social Behavior. *Television and growing up: The impact of televised violence.* Washington: U.S. Government Printing Office.

A survey of children's radio preferences. (1940, July 13). *School and Society.* p. 23.

Terrace, V. (1979). *Complete encyclopedia of television programs, 1947-1979.* (Vols. 1 & 2). South Brunswick, NJ: A. S. Barnes.

Terrace, V. (1981). *Radio's golden years: The encyclopedia of radio programs, 1930-1960.* San Diego: A. S. Barnes.

Time-Life (1969). *This fabulous century, 1930-1940.* (Vol. 4). New York: Time-Life Books.

Turow, J. (1981). *Entertainment, education and the hard sell: Three decades of network children's television.* New York: Praeger.

Uncle Don's radio birthday. (1940, December 16). *Newsweek,* p. 52.

Whipple, J. (1938). *How to write for radio.* New York: Whittlesey House.

Whiteside, T. (1947, March 5). Up, up and away. *New Republic,* pp. 15-17.

Wylie, M. (1939). *Radio writing.* New York: Farrar & Rinehart.

Wylie, M. (1940). *Best broadcasts of 1939-1940.* New York: Whittlesey House.

APPENDIX A

Programs with Network, Years Broadcast,
and Regular Characters

1. *The Adventures of Dick Cole.*
   Syndicated, 30 minutes, 1942.
   Dick Cole, Simba Carna, Major Farr.

2. *The Adventures of Frank Merriwell.*
   NBC, 15 minutes in mid-1930's; 30 minutes
   1946-1949.
   Frank Merriwell, Bart Hodge, Inza Burrage.

3. *The Adventures of Superman.*
   Syndicated, 15 minutes, 1939; Mutual 1940-1949;
   ABC 1949-1951.
   Clark Kent (Superman), Lois Lane, Jimmy Olson,
   Editor Perry White.

4. *The Air Adventures of Jimmy Allen.*
   Syndicated, 15 minutes, 1933-1936; re-released in
   early 1940's.
   Jimmy Allen, Speed Robertson, Flash Lewis.

5. *The American School of the Air.*
   CBS, 30 minutes, 1930-1948.

6. *Bobby Benson and the B-Bar-B Riders.*
   CBS, 15 minutes, 1932-1936; Mutual, 30 minutes,
   1949-1955.
   Bobby Benson, Tex Mason, Windy Wales, Harka
   the Indian, Diogenes Dodwaddle, Polly Armstead,
   Aunt Lilly, Irish.

7. *Buck Rogers in the 25th Century.*
   CBS, 15 minutes, 1932-1936; 15 minutes, 30 minutes, 1939-1947.
   Buck Rogers, Wilma Deering, Dr. Huer, Black Barney, Killer Kane.

8. *Captain Midnight.*
   Mutual, 15 minutes, 1940-1949.
   Captain Midnight, Chuck Ramsey, Joyce Ryan, Ichabod Mudd, Ivan Shark.

9. *Chandu, the Magician.*
   Mutual, 15 minutes, 1932-1936; Mutual, ABC, 30 minutes, 1948-1950.
   Frank Chandler (Chandu), Dorothy Regent, Betty Regent, Bob Regent, Princess Nadji, Roxor.

10. *The Cinnamon Bear.*
    Syndicated, 15 minutes, 1937-1950's.
    Paddy O'Cinnamon, Judy Barton, Jimmy Barton, Crazy Quilt Dragon, Wintergreen Witch, FeFo the Giant, Melissa.

11. *The Cisco Kid.*
    Mutual, 30 minutes, 1942-1950's.
    Cisco Kid, Pancho.

12. *Dick Tracy.*
    Mutual, 15 minutes, 1935-1937; NBC, 1937-1939; ABC, 1943-1948.
    Dick Tracy, Pat Patton, Tess Trueheart, Junior, Chief Brandon.

13. *Don Winslow of the Navy.*
    NBC Blue, 15 minutes, 1937-1939; 30 minutes
    1942-1945.
    Commander Don Winslow, Lt. Red Pennington,
    Mercedes Colby.

14. *Dorothy Gordon.*
    Mutual, 15 minutes, 1938-1939.
    Dorothy Gordon.

15. *Flash Gordon.*
    Mutual, 15 minutes, 1935-1936.
    Flash Gordon, Dale Arden, Dr. Hans Zarkoff,
    Prince Barin, Thun, Ming the Merciless.

16. *Gene Autry's Melody Ranch.*
    CBS, 15 minutes, 30 minutes, 1940-1956.
    Gene Autry, Pat Buttram, Cass County Boys, Gene
    Autry Blue Jeans, Carl Cotner's Melody Ranch
    Hardway Six.

17. *The Green Hornet.*
    Mutual, 30 minutes, 1938-1939; NBC Blue,
    1939-1952.
    Britt Reid (The Green Hornet), Kato, Mike Axford,
    Lenore Case, Ed Lowry, Editor Gunnigan.

18. *Hoofbeats.*
    Syndicated, 15 minutes, 1937.
    Buck Jones, the Old Wrangler.

19. *Hop Harrigan.*
    NBC Blue, 15 minutes, 1942-1946; Mutual,
    1946-1948.
    Hop Harrigan, Tank Tinker, Gale Nolan.

20. *Hopalong Cassidy.*
    Mutual, CBS, 30 minutes, 1950-1952.
    Hopalong Cassidy, California Carlson.

21. *Jack Armstrong, the All-American Boy.*
    CBS, 15 minutes, 1933-1936; NBC Blue, 15
    minutes, 1936-1947; 30 minutes, 1947-1950.
    Jack Armstrong, Uncle Jim Fairfield, Betty
    Fairfield, Bob Fairfield.

22. *Jungle Jim.*
    Syndicated, 15 minutes, probably late 1930's.
    Jungle Jim Bradley, Kolu, Shanghai Lil DeVille.

23. *Let's Pretend.*
    CBS, 30 minutes, 1930-1954.
    Uncle Bill Adams, Host.

24. *Little Orphan Annie.*
    NBC Blue, Mutual, 15 minutes, 1931-1943.
    Annie, Sandy the Dog, Oliver "Daddy" Warbucks,
    Joe Corntassel, Punjab, the Asp.

25. *The Lone Ranger.*
    Mutual, 30 minutes, 1933-1954.
    The Lone Ranger, Tonto, Dan Reid.

26. *Mark Trail.*
    Mutual, 30 minutes, 1950-1951; ABC, 15 minutes,
    1951-1952.
    Mark Trail, Scotty, Cherry, Andy the Dog.

27. *No School Today.*
    ABC, 90 minute, 2 hours, 1950-1954.
    Big Jon Arthur, Sparkie

28. *Popeye the Sailor.*
     NBC, CBS, 15 minutes, 1935-1936.
     Popeye, Matey, Olive Oyl, J. Wellington Wimpy,
     Bluto.

29. *Red Ryder.*
     NBC Blue, Mutual, 30 minutes, 1942-1950's.
     Red Ryder, Little Beaver, Aunt Duchess.

30. *Renfrew of the Mounted.*
     CBS, 15 minutes, 1936-1937; NBC Blue, 30
     minutes, 1937-1940.
     Inspector Douglas Renfrew.

31. *Rin Tin Tin.*
     NBC Blue, 15 minutes, 1930-1934; Mutual, 30
     minutes, 1955-1956.
     Rin Tin Tin, Rusty, Lt. Rick Masters.

32. *The Roy Rogers Show.*
     Mutual, NBC, 30 minutes, 1944-1955.
     Roy Rogers, Dale Evans, Gabby Hayes, Pat Brady,
     Sons of the Pioneers, Riders of the Purple Sage, the
     Mellow Men.

33. *Sergeant Preston of the Yukon.*
     Mutual, 15 minutes, 1939-1947; Mutual, ABC, 30
     minutes, 1947-1955.
     Sergeant Preston, King the Dog.

34. *The Singing Lady.*
     NBC Blue, 15 minutes, 1932-1950's.
     Ireene Wicker.

35. *Skippy.*
    NBC, 15 minutes, 1931; CBS, 1932-1935.
    Skippy, Sooky, Carole.

36. *Sky King.*
    ABC, 15 minutes, 1946; 30 minutes, 1947-1950;
    Mutual, 1950-1954.
    Sky King, Clipper, Penny.

37. *Smilin' Ed's Buster Brown Gang.*
    NBC, 30 minutes, 1944-1952.
    Ed McConnell, Squeaky the Mouse, Midnight the Cat,
    Froggie the Gremlin, Grandie the Piano, Alkali Pete
    the Cowboy, Buster Brown, Tige the Dog.

38. *Smilin' Jack.*
    Mutual, 15 minutes, 1939.
    Jack Martin, Mary, Fat Stuff, Downwind Jackson,
    Dixie.

39. *Space Patrol.*
    ABC, 30 minutes, 1950-1955.
    Buzz Corey, Captain Happy.

40. *Straight Arrow.*
    Mutual, 30 minutes, 1948-1951.
    Steve Adams (Straight Arrow), Packy.

41. *Tennessee Jed.*
    ABC, 15 minutes, 1945-1947.
    Jed Sloan, Cookstove, Snake, José, Sheriff Tate.

42. *Terry and the Pirates.*
    NBC, 15 minutes, 1937-1939, 1943-1948.
    Terry Lee, Patrick Ryan, Big Stoop, Hot Shot Charlie,
    Connie the Coolie, Burma, the Dragon Lady.

43. *Tom Corbett, Space Cadet.*
    ABC, 30 minutes, 1952.
    Tom Corbett, Roger Manning, Captain Strong, Astro.

44. *The Tom Mix Ralston Straightshooters.*
    NBC, 15 minutes, 1933-1949; Mutual, 30 minutes, 1949-1950.
    Tom Mix, Mike Shaw, Wash.

45. *Uncle Don.*
    WOR, Mutual, 15 minutes, 1928 or 1929-1949.
    Don Carney, Willipus Wollipus, Suzan Beduzin, Huzen Beduzin.

46. *Wild Bill Hickok.*
    Mutual, 30 minutes, 1951-1956.
    Wild Bill Hickok, Jingles P. Jones.

47. *Wilderness Road.*
    CBS, 15 minutes, 1936-1937.
    Daniel Boone, the Weston Family, Bunch Flowers.